TO MY PARENTS

THE AMERICAN PREDICAMENT

The American Predicament

Apartheid and United States Foreign Policy

A.M. THOMAS
Senior Lecturer in International Relations
Mahatma Gandhi University, Kottayam

Routledge
Taylor & Francis Group
LONDON AND NEW YORK

First published 1997 by Ashgate Publishing

Reissued 2018 by Routledge
2 Park Square, Milton Park, Abingdon, Oxon, OX14 4RN
52 Vanderbilt Avenue, New York, NY 10017

Routledge is an imprint of the Taylor & Francis Group, an informa business

A Library of Congress record exists under LC control number: 97071459

ISBN 13: 978-1-138-39020-1 (hbk)
ISBN 13: 978-1-138-39021-8 (pbk)
ISBN 13: 978-0-429-42345-1 (ebk)

Contents

List of Tables

Preface

Most Americans believe that the United States has a unique mission in the world–to set an example to others not only how a country ought to be governed but also how it should conduct its foreign relations. The vision of the "city upon a hill" remains with Americans to this day. Americans also regard their country to be the champion of ideals like equality, liberty and justice. The spirit and philosophy of these ideals were reflected not only in the Declaration of Independence, the Constitution and the Gettysburg Address, but also in the speeches and writings of most American leaders. The observance of these ideals was urged both in domestic political life as well as in the conduct of foreign relations. Moreover, these values were thought to have universal applicability, and other nations were exhorted to adhere to them. It is in this regard that South Africa posed a serious dilemma to the United States. Apartheid, the doctrine of racialism which was based on the idea of the superiority of the White race, had been practised for decades in South Africa. The policy of apartheid was devised by the White minority to ensure its survival and protect itself against unanticipated vicissitudes. Segregation and discrimination were observed in all walks of life and enforced by legislation. For the non-Whites who constituted the majority, its impact was disastrous and deprived them of any control over their lives.

For several decades apartheid remained a familiar and oft-quoted word in international circles, one which touched the conscience and stirred the passions of millions around the world. It became the subject of debate in hundreds of forums and incurred the opprobrium of the civilised world. While the rest of the world had accepted the idea of racial equality, South Africa gave racial discrimination a philosophical basis and legal sanction. South Africa not only discriminated against certain sections of its population and deprived them of their basic human rights but also sought to justify this on the grounds that separation of races was natural.

Defenders of apartheid questioned the rationale of South Africa alone being criticised for discriminating against its citizens. They cited countless instances of discrimination and denial of rights by states against individuals and groups on ethnic and other grounds. It is true that cases of discrimination and persecution exist elsewhere in the world. Moreover, in any society there is often some degree of inequality. But it would be illogical to compare these cases with the South African one. In none of the other countries had the principle of racial inequality been legally enshrined. Inequality has often been the product of history, but it has not been justified or perpetuated for that reason. Pseudo-racial theories have been propounded from time to time, but no modern state has accepted them, apart from instances like that of Nazi Germany. Apartheid was one of the most noxious forms assumed by slavery in modern times and constituted one of the most severe and atrocious violations of human rights. South Africa sought to insulate itself from international opinion and opprobrium. It resisted global efforts on the ground that its policies were a domestic concern and that such efforts constituted an interference in its internal affairs. The international community on the other hand regarded apartheid no longer a domestic concern but one with international dimensions and repercussions. Furthermore, in the case of South Africa it was widely acknowledged that the case for racial justice transcended the claims of international law.

Apartheid thus being undeniably the antithesis of American ideals, the United States was naturally expected to oppose it in unequivocal terms. However, the United States had significant tangible interests, specifically economic and strategic, in South Africa, which played a decisive role in shaping American policy. South Africa had the most developed economy in the entire African continent and was the repository of several important minerals. Its geographic and strategic location was also of great importance to the United States. Consequently, the entire issue placed the United States in a predicament. On the one hand it had to adhere to its ideals, while on the other refrain from alienating the South African regime and damaging its interests. Whichever course it resorted to, there were corresponding repercussions.

It is in this context that a study of American responses–of perceptions and policies towards South Africa–assumes significance. There had always been an intense debate during the days of apartheid over United States policy towards South Africa. This book endeavours to examine United States policy towards South Africa in the broader context of American ideals and responses to apartheid. In order to facilitate a thorough analysis, the focus of the book has been limited to the nineteen seventies, or more precisely from 1969 to 1980, covering a period of three administrations, those of Nixon, Ford and Carter.

The developments within South Africa were largely ignored by American administrations for a long time. However, during the nineteen fifties, with apartheid becoming an issue of international concern, and the question being raised at the United Nations, the United States began displaying some interest in the racial crisis in South Africa. With the Sharpville massacre of 1960, when about seventy Blacks were killed in police firing, American interest was suddenly kindled, but the following decade was witness to mere verbal interventionism rather than concrete measures. At the United Nations, the United States supported mildly worded resolutions and half-measures, but continued its relations with South Africa unhindered. The international demand for economic sanctions against South Africa always found one of its foremost opponents in the United States. Maintaining cordial relations with South Africa, notwithstanding the nature of the apartheid system, was considered to be in the best interests of the United States. Thus by 1968 the failure of any sincere American effort to address the South African issue was evident.

The period under study was particularly significant for the United States both in the domestic and international spheres. The beginning of the nineteen seventies witnessed an increasing interest and articulation on South African issues within the United States, particularly by Afro-Americans who had just achieved civil and voting rights. At the international level, with the advent of détente and the relaxation of tensions, the United States could focus more attention on problems like that of apartheid in South Africa.

In writing this book I have received the help of several individuals, all of whom I may not be able to mention here, but to whom I nevertheless remain grateful. I am indebted to Prof. C. V. Cheriyan for his advice and constant encouragement. I am also grateful to Prof. Tom Travis of Bucknell University for meticulously reading and commenting on every aspect of the initial draft; to my colleagues, Ramachandra, Seethi, Raju, Ramakrishnan and Harilal; and to my students at the School of International Relations; for their support and co-operation. A special word of appreciation goes to the staff of the American Studies Research Centre, Hyderabad; American Center Library, Madras; the libraries of the Mahatma Gandhi University, Kottayam; University of Kerala, Trivandrum; Jawaharlal Nehru University, New Delhi and the United Nations Information Centre, New Delhi. Grateful acknowledgement is made to the United States Information Agency, Washington, DC and the United States Information Service, Madras for nominating me to the International Visitor Program on Decision Making in United States Foreign Policy, which gave me a better insight into the intricacies of American foreign policy. A special word of thanks goes to Ms. Valerie Saunders and Ms. Ann Newell of Ashgate Publishing Limited for their advice in the preparation of this book, and to Benny and Anil of M/s Copy Write, Ettumanoor, for their painstaking and efficient word processing work. This book would have remained a distant dream without the support of the members of my family. My wife Teresa was the most important reader and critic of the manuscript and my debt to her is incalculable. And finally a word of thanks to my daughter Annie, whose demands on me to narrate fairy tales provided a pleasant respite from the tales of the real world. For any shortcomings of this book, I remain solely responsible.

A. M. Thomas

1 American Ideals, Apartheid and United States Foreign Policy

Throughout their history Americans have constantly eulogised ideals or values like equality, liberty and democracy. They have advocated the application of these ideals in all spheres of social and political activity including domestic politics and foreign relations. Racial issues like that of apartheid in South Africa became of concern to the United States since they were the antithesis of what are commonly referred to as American ideals. The very genesis of the United States was based on these ideals which Gunnar Myrdal called the "American Creed". The Declaration of Independence proclaimed that "we hold these truths to be self-evident, that all men are created equal, that they are endowed by their Creator with certain inalienable rights, that among these are life, liberty and the pursuit of happiness". The same sentiments echo in the Constitution and the Bill of Rights. The Preamble to the Constitution states that the rationale for creating the state was to form a more perfect union, to establish among other things, justice; promote the general welfare and secure the blessings of liberty. In his Gettysburg Address, Lincoln proclaimed that the nation was conceived in liberty and dedicated to the proposition that all men are created equal.

Although there are differences of opinion on the precise ideals of the American society, there appears to be a general agreement that equality, liberty and democracy are among them. The dominant political creed of the United States is in essence the seventeenth century liberal philosophy of John Locke, who is considered the ideological godfather of the American Revolution. His writings on natural rights constituted the political gospel of most educated Americans in the late eighteenth century. Locke believed that the role of government was a limited one, intended to protect an individual's life, liberty and property. Governments owed their existence to popular consent and were regulated by established laws. Lockean philosophy has become an integral part of American life. Hartz (1955, p.10) states that while it is a symbol of rationalism in the entire West, the American devotion to it has been "so irrational".

Equality and liberty were very appealing concepts to early Americans. By mentioning equality first, the Declaration of Independence perhaps gave it greater importance than liberty.[1] It was a moral declaration where Thomas Jefferson asserted that everyone is politically equal, that governments can receive power legitimately only from the people and the only justification of government is to secure the right of the people to life, liberty and the pursuit of happiness. Moreover, when Jefferson penned the classic and immortal phrases of the Declaration, the equality so affirmed was that of "all men". "No restrictions, exclusions or barriers were contemplated" (Lipson, 1964, p.97). In the early decades of the nineteenth century, Alexis de Tocqueville observed that there was a great degree of equality in the United States. He begins his treatise *Democracy in America* thus:

> No novelty in the United States struck me more vividly during my stay there than the equality of conditions. It was easy to see the immense influence of this basic fact on the whole course of society. It gives a particular turn to public opinion and a particular twist to the laws, new maxims to those who govern and particular habits to the governed. (Tocqueville, 1966, p.3)

But Americans of the late eighteenth century or the nineteenth century had not made the principle of equality applicable to all inhabitants of the United States. Liberty too remained, in the post civil war years, as before, a complex, many sided and ambiguous term. Burns (1990, p.121) states that even in the nineteen thirties, the idea of liberty or freedom was "still more a source of ambivalence than of coherence in the American consciousness". Americans also believe that their ideals are not meant for them alone, but for non-Americans too. They have consistently emphasised that their ideals extend to other people and countries. Donald Kagan (1983, p.88) states:

> (W)e Americans have been raised in the tradition of our Declaration of Independence and our Bill of Rights. It is natural for us to assume that our rights are inevitable and to apply them universally, for if they are not valid for all mankind, how can they be valid for us?

In essence, American ideals reflect and represent the highest at an ethical level. There is a strong moral dimension to the whole issue of ideals. Ideals are considered standards to be observed in the conduct of political relations, both at home and abroad.

A Domestic Moral Concern

But as history shows, it has been in the sphere of the racial question in the United States that American ideals became a domestic moral concern. Until the mid eighteen sixties, slavery existed as a pillar of American society, as the antithesis of liberty and equality.[2] The existence of slavery was not compatible with the American self image of a chosen people engaged in a grand experiment. The rhetoric of ideals was meaningless in the face of such a national disgrace. Tocqueville had observed:

> If there ever are great revolutions there, they will be caused by the presence of the blacks upon American soil. That is to say, it will not be the equality of social conditions but rather their inequality which may give rise thereto. (Tocqueville, 1966, p.614)

Neither the emancipation of slaves during the Civil War, nor the constitutional amendments of the Reconstruction era improved the lot of the Afro-Americans. The Supreme Court in its verdict of 1896, in the *Plessy v. Ferguson* case upheld the idea that "separate was equal". In the interwar period racial problems that were confined to the South spread elsewhere. In 1944, during the course of World War II, when the United States was projecting itself as the champion of freedom in the world, Gunnar Myrdal wrote *An American Dilemma*, a study prepared for the Carnegie Foundation. The fundamental thesis of the work was that there was a tension between American ideals and reality. He highlighted the enormous gap that existed between the core values of America like moral concern, liberalism, rationalism, freedom and equality of opportunity on the one hand and the inequality and discrimination that existed in the United States on the other. For Myrdal (1962), the American dilemma was the perpetual conflict between all that constituted the American creed and the increasing prejudice against particular individuals or types of people.

The post-war period was eventful for race relations in the United States. The fifties and sixties witnessed the Afro-American struggle for civil rights, the Supreme Court's verdict against segregation in the *Brown v.*

Board of Education case and the governmental efforts to grant Afro-Americans civil and voting rights.[3] Despite tremendous changes in the lives of Afro-Americans, problems remain unresolved. Discrimination still exists at some levels. Although they are legally equal, they are woefully behind economically and in the general condition of their lives. In some fundamental respects they are now equal participants in the political system. But in a more subtle sense, they are not able to participate fully. There is still considerable prejudice against them, they are frequently not afforded the educational advantages that the average citizen avails of and too often are deprived of the opportunities of better health and medical care. Economically their progress has been less significant than in politics and education. Above all, within themselves they are facing a sharp class bifurcation–a prospering middle class and a devastated underclass (Graham, 1990, p.453). Manning Marable (1985, p.74) writes that "to be Black in America is to live within a fundamental contradiction which rests between the promise of democracy and the harsh reality of racial inequality".

It is surprising, paradoxical and tragic as well that a nation founded on the principle that all men are created equal should be riddled with a race problem. In precise terms, the racial problem is not just one for Afro-Americans alone, but for all Americans; a moral dilemma that strikes at the roots of American democracy.

Ideals and Foreign Policy

Erwin D. Canham, editor of the *Christian Science Monitor*, while delivering the Paul Anthony Brick Lectures pointed out that what Americans seek as a nation is the opportunity for all men to choose their own forms of government freely, to set up institutions of their choice, and to strive for the fulfilment of their destinies in ways resultant from their own capacities, potentialities and ideals (Canham, 1964, p.6). While discussing foreign policy goals, Samuel P. Huntington (1982, pp.18-19) states that the desire of most Americans was that the structure and functioning of their foreign policy institutions should reflect liberal values. They also expected American foreign policy to be substantively directed to the promotion of these values in the external environment. Furthermore, foreign policy goals should reflect not only the security concerns of the nation and economic interests of groups within the country, but also the political values and principles that define American identity. "If these values do define foreign policy goals, then that policy is morally justified, the opponents of that policy at home and abroad are morally illegitimate, and all efforts must be directed toward overcoming the opponents and achieving the goals". The idea of a unique American mission has been an important theme in United States foreign policy. More than most nationalities, Americans have thought of themselves as destined to bring the blessings of liberty and self-government to the less fortunate parts of the world. Osgood (1953, p.7) observes that the most commonly preferred among the national ends related to the fundamental ideals of Western civilisation are those principles of right conduct which apply to personal relations. This means that ideals are not only an important concern in the realm of foreign policy but that they have a strong moral content. It also raises the question whether a policy based on a moral consideration can be pursued at the expense of a country's other interests. Stupak (1976, p.20) observes that moralism has been the guiding principle, ethics the underlying concern, while liberty, peace and democracy the ultimate ends of American foreign policy. He also states:

> To Americans foreign policy was thought to be the cosmic struggle between right and wrong; the perpetual repulsion of tyranny; the true belief in individual liberty, freedom and equality; total dedication to the rule of law; and peaceful settlement of disputes with an ethical, democratic, missionary zeal undergirded with intense moral idealism.

In this context, the extent to which the United States can uphold these ideals in foreign policy, and the degree to which they would be in conflict with its other national interests becomes an issue for discussion. It has been asserted that as the United States by virtue of its immense power had been thrust into an inescapable position of world leadership, it had to invariably face more and more decisions in which it had to compromise with its ideals in the short run in order to achieve them in the long run. Furthermore, the more conscious America became of the need for defending and promoting its ideals, the more acute this dilemma came to be. Americans would be plagued as never before by the seeming inconsistency between their ideals and their actions (Osgood, 1953, p.438).

On the other hand it may be argued that moral action by a state would be meaningless if it *always* demanded a sacrificial or suicidal posture, for then only angels or saints could act morally. Moral action on the part of an individual or nation, it may be said, does not require self-restraint to the point of self-destruction, but it allows the pursuit of one's interests provided such interests are subjected to rational examination and provided they are related to the interests of others over a long period of time. Charles Frankel (1975, p.61) points out that American political and moral principles are not applicable or wanted everywhere. Even if they were applicable and wanted, they would still be beyond human powers to implement everywhere. Kagan (1983, p.88) also maintains that to assume that the rights Americans enjoy are universal, is natural but unjustified. There is no basis, he says, to apply them to all humans.

What then can the extent be to which the United States can interact with another state on the basis of its ideals? Advocates of the strict observance of ideals in foreign policy would call for stringent action against countries which violate them. Critics of this approach will question its rationale on the grounds that a foreign policy committed to normal relations only with virtuous regimes that protect human rights and to hostility towards governments that violate them would be either excessively dangerous or hypocritical. They point out that most regimes in existence have violated the American notion of human rights to a considerable degree and a nation that holds on steadfastly to such an idealist policy will have few friends and many enemies. American foreign policy, to this day, has been tormented by the pulls in opposite directions of these two approaches.

Apartheid in South Africa

The ideals that Americans upheld were being violated in South Africa where the Blacks who formed 73 per cent of the population were oppressed in their own land.[4] A White minority which was in control of the country dictated the fate of the majority. Ever since Europeans began settling in that part of the African continent, Blacks were through different means controlled by a system created and dominated by the former. In the early days of European settlement, land was abundant and its acquisition by the newcomers did not pose a serious problem for the Hottentots and Bushmen who constituted the indigenous population. The problem of land ownership cropped up as the Europeans advanced eastward and northward to areas densely populated by the Bantu peoples. The British government which was then in control decided to create reserves for the natives during the second half of the nineteenth century. In some parts of South Africa, White settlers occupied land at their own discretion without any concern for the requirements of the Black population. In other parts the native population was largely exterminated or displaced through war.

For the Europeans, the creation of reserves provided great advantages. It protected their areas from possible encroachment by the Blacks who were denied access there except as wage earners and tenant labourers. By placing restrictions on the area of land available as reserves, the Europeans were able to force large numbers of Blacks off the land. The consequence of this non-availability of land for Blacks was their reliance on Whites who could provide them work in return for low wages. Again, by deliberately creating small units of non-contiguous land within large areas and designating them homelands, the Whites destroyed the unity, solidarity and social cohesion of the Blacks. Finally the reserves served as "shock absorbers", where aged and infirm Blacks could retire once they were no longer in a position to offer their labour, without being a liability on the state (Boateng, 1978, pp.164-167).

The South African policy of apartheid is usually traced to 1948, but its foundations were laid much earlier. As land came to be controlled by the Whites, their grip on other aspects of life became easier. Blacks were reduced to a permanent proletarian class and exploited as a labour force in agriculture and mining. The traditional social structure of the Blacks was shattered. Laws ensuring the inequality between the Blacks and Whites were enshrined in the written law of the land. The Blacks were deprived of their livelihood except their labour which was adjudged cheap by the Whites. Thus by 1948, segregation and subjugation of the Blacks was already in existence.

The hardening attitude of the South African regime against the Blacks assumed its most dramatic and vicious form in 1948 when Prime Minister D. F. Malan summed up the new Nationalist government's racial policy as one of *apartheid,* an Afrikaans word meaning "separateness". By this policy, the government was determined to bring about a complete separation of the Whites and non-Whites based on the obnoxious doctrine of the racial superiority of the Whites and a deliberate attempt was made to prevent any kind of fusion of the different sections of the non-White population.

The singular characteristic of the apartheid era that began in 1948 was the introduction of a more rigorous, systematic, comprehensive and strictly enforced control by the state over the Blacks as far as their movement to urban areas and their employment and residential opportunities were concerned. What distinguished apartheid legislation was that "the previous ad hoc segregationist measures were amended, supplemented and combined within a political ideology that has been pursued with a single-mindedness of purpose" (Browett, 1982, pp.20-21).

From 1948 onwards the South African government brought into existence numerous laws which were aimed at keeping the Blacks in a state of perpetual bondage and subjugation. The philosophical tenets of apartheid were formulated in a manner to protect the Whites from any ideology, policy or attack that could endanger or undermine their continued domination. To ensure this, separation had to be effected at all levels. This, the regime discovered, could be achieved through impregnable legal barriers as well as physical distance and the imponderable force of custom. Magubane (1979, p.222) writes:

> Throughout history those classes that exploit and dominate others have tried to find theoretical and ideological weapons to supplement their physical domination. They propagate these ideologies in all the institutions of society in order to convince themselves and the oppressed classes that inequality is inevitable, the natural state of human society.

The Whites who had found a permanent abode in South Africa aimed at denying national status and citizenship to the indigenous population. The settlers therefore sought a theoretical justification for their actions and designed laws which rejected the principle of racial equality and encouraged separate development. Under the *Population Registration Act 1950*, the central racial classification law, sometimes described as the cornerstone of apartheid, every person was assigned to one of the races. John Dugard (1978, pp.62-63) states that this act was par excellence an example of a statute which conferred humiliation and a sense of inferiority among those who were obliged to submit to investigation into their family history, social habits and physical experience. He further states:

> What could be more humiliating than an enquiry into the precise racial admixture of one's parents, the colour of one's friends one keeps and the extent to which one's hair, fingernails, lips and other physical features incline towards Caucasian or Negroid?

The country was racially divided according to the *Group Areas Act 1950* which provided for the establishment of racial ghettos in which ownership and occupation of land were restricted to a specified population group. Eighty seven per cent of the land was allotted to the Whites who constituted only eighteen per cent of the population and the remaining land was divided among the Blacks. The native reserves were called homelands or bantustans. The homelands policy also known as grand apartheid envisaged the separate development of South Africa's Blacks. Homelands were created out of the existing 264 African reserves. The policy reached its peak in 1976 with the granting of "independence" to Transkei.

The homelands policy had been criticised on several grounds. One criticism was that by giving great emphasis on tribal divisions which were on the wane, the government could pursue a policy of divide and rule. Another was that the non-contiguous territories supposed to be the tribal homelands were poor substitutes for the original tribal lands. The strongest criticism was that the homelands policy was based on the fiction that Blacks residing in the White areas were temporary workers rather than a permanent and integral part of South African society. "Viewed in this light", the homelands policy became "a device for assuring a continuing supply of African labour while avoiding the granting of full political, civil, economic and social rights to the African workers and their families" (*South Africa: Time Running Out*, 1981, p.51).

Laws were enacted to permit the government to label almost any activity it disapproved of as illegal, with strong enforcement procedures. The *Suppression of Communism Act, 1950* (later renamed *Internal Security Act* and amended in 1976 and 1982) covered organisations and individuals who engaged in activities which would endanger the security of the state and the maintenance of public order.

To keep racial lines from blurring further, marriage and sexual relations between Blacks and Whites were proscribed through the *Prohibition of Mixed Marriages Act, 1949* and the *Immorality Act* of 1950 and 1957. The *Reservation of Separate Amenities Act, 1953* allowed any person in control of public premises to reserve separate and unequal facilities for different races and placed curbs on the power of the courts to declare such reservations invalid. This resulted in separate and unequal amenities for different races in all spheres of life–public conveyance, restaurants, libraries and parks to mention but a few of the more obvious facilities. The apparatus of apartheid was enriched by a plethora of laws which were designed to be all encompassing, all pervading and affecting all aspects of South African life.[5] As Graham Leach (1987, p.70) observed, apartheid was:

> . . . not just about which races can sit in which train compartments, who can visit which cinema, who can use which lavatory. It is about the way

> a whole society is organized. What has happened in South Africa since 1948 represents some of the most formidable social engineering that the twentieth century has witnessed, a system that has set in progress vast movements of population, that has led to hundreds of thousands of people being uprooted, that has created an army of functionaries whose task it is to enforce the whole order. It is a system of government founded upon a master-plan, which, because it is based on colour, has aroused the opprobrium of the world. . . .

The theory and practice of apartheid were no doubt far removed from human reasoning and will remain a scar on human civilisation. In his autobiography, *Long Walk to Freedom*, Nelson Mandela writes that the policy of apartheid created such a deep and lasting wound in his country that his people would spend years if not generations recovering from it (Mandela, 1994, p.614). Apartheid was indeed a crime against humanity and morally reprehensible. Arthur Schlesinger, Jr. (1986, pp.81-82) states that there are certain international questions with so clear a moral character that moral judgement must guide political judgement. Racial justice is one of them.

Apartheid: An American Foreign Policy Dilemma

It was towards such a situation in South Africa that the United States was reacting – towards a society that was multiracial as its own, but where racial discrimination was legalised. There was a strong moral issue involved and the question was raised as to what United States policy towards a country practising racial discrimination should be. The policy was also influenced to a large extent by United States economic and strategic interests in South Africa. It was not the first time that the United States was confronting such an issue. As early as 1913 the Woodrow Wilson administration had refused to recognise the Victoriano Huerta regime in Mexico on moralistic grounds. Wilson justified his policy thus:

> We dare not turn from the principle that morality and not expediency is the thing that must guide us and that we will never condone iniquity because it is most convenient to do so. . . . It is a very perilous thing to determine the foreign policy of a nation in terms of material interest. It not only is unfair to those with whom you are dealing, but it is degrading as regards your own actions. (Bailey, 1990, p.556)

In the United States there always existed a broad consensus not only that respect for human rights should form an integral element in international relations, but that it should form the cornerstone of American foreign policy. Liberal opinion particularly regarded the prudent, passive and ambiguous policy of the United States on apartheid to be unjustifiable. "From an ideological perspective, it contravened America's avowed belief in principles like democracy, freedom and equality, making a mockery of the nation's claim to lead the 'free world' " (Crabb, 1976, p.61).

In the nineteen seventies, South Africa had developed into a serious foreign policy issue for the United States. When it came to deal with apartheid, the United States was engaged in verbal interventionism, one in which there was high sounding rhetoric, critical of apartheid and the South African regime. But when it came to concrete measures like the imposition of economic sanctions, the United States backtracked. Apartheid was totally against whatever the nation claimed it stood for. South Africa became an area where United States foreign policy faced a dilemma–the inability to do what it proclaimed to the world. The American predicament was thus concerning United States policy towards apartheid and South Africa. On the one hand policy had to reflect American ideals and on the other, such a policy was expected not to be detrimental to its economic and strategic interests.

Notes

1. In writing the Declaration of Independence, Jefferson was influenced not only by the philosophy of Locke but also by the English heritage, with its traditional concern for the rights of man; and by the colonial experience itself.
2. At the Philadelphia Convention where the Constitution was drafted the issue of slavery cropped up. The question of its abolition was not pursued for the sake of the more urgent goal of a strong national government.
3. The Supreme Court verdict in the *Brown v. Board of Education* case overruled the verdict in the *Plessy v. Ferguson* case. The 1954 verdict in the Brown case said that "separate facilities are inherently unequal".
4. In the late nineteen seventies the population of South Africa by ethnic composition was: Blacks, 73.09 per cent; Whites, 14.29 per cent; Coloured, 9.74 per cent; and Asians, 2.85 per cent.
5. Only a few from the long list of apartheid laws have been mentioned here.

2 United States Interests in South Africa

South Africa's economic and strategic importance for the United States has been a much debated subject. This was particularly so during the nineteen seventies and eighties when United States policy towards South Africa came to be increasingly scrutinised and questioned. In the post-war period there was a significant change in the nature and extent of American involvement in global affairs. If isolationism was previously a factor that kept the United States away from any region, it no longer remained so. South Africa, although a part of the long neglected Africa, had carved out a special position for itself as one of the more important regional powers. The focus of this chapter will be on the extent of South Africa's importance to the United States in the nineteen seventies. More precisely it will concentrate on the political dimensions of United States policy towards South Africa, South Africa's economic power, American trade with and investment in South Africa, South African mineral resources and the strategic importance of South Africa.

The Cold War and Southern Africa

In the post-war period, the major influence on American foreign policy was the objective of the containment of Communism. In the initial years of this period, Africa was not a major concern for the United States since most of the countries there were still colonies of its European allies. Thomas J. Noer (1981, p.271) states that an essay on United States relations with Black Africa could be titled "the invisible chapter" in any book. Only in the wake of independence and the subsequent Soviet and Chinese penetration of the continent did the United States start displaying any concern of significance. The United States perceived global and regional issues in the light of the East-West conflict. Consequently, American policy towards a region was shaped *inter alia* by the consideration of how much it would assist in the struggle against Communism. Both the United States and South Africa were anti-Communist, they believed in the maintenance of the status quo in the global distribution of power and were opposed to violent and unregulated change. South Africa on its part was willing to join the United States against the Soviet Union and serve as a regional surrogate.

Most liberation movements in Southern Africa regarded the Soviet Union as a supporter of the cause of racial justice and a provider of arms for their struggle. Soviet behaviour towards such movements was quite consistent with the writings and speeches of Soviet leaders and academics (Golan, 1988). In the ongoing struggle against the West, Soviet strategists placed much emphasis on the strategic importance of South Africa. Moreover, the liberation of South Africa with their support would have strengthened the military position of the Soviet Union in the world at large (Gann and Duignan, 1981, p.197). By intervening in Southern Africa the Soviet Union hoped to make strategic, economic and political gains at the expense of the West particularly the United States. While exporting Communist ideology, Moscow also sought to safeguard its future access to the raw materials of the region as well as its military bases. Another Soviet objective was to weaken China's influence in the area. The balance of power had begun to change in Africa and "Marxism-Leninism, far from being an exiles' creed had become a continental challenge to the West" (Duignan and Gann, 1984, p.293). Southern Africa was also central to Moscow's image in the Third World. To spread its political and economic influence in a manner consistent with its role as a world power was one of the Soviet objectives. Another objective which was related to this was to diminish or eliminate western influence and control in Africa. The Soviet Union had come to realise that in the post Vietnam period the United States would not be prepared to take risks in defending positions that were not vital. The Soviet perception was strengthened during the events that arose in the nineteen seventies following the Portuguese decolonization. Following the Portuguese withdrawal, pro-Soviet groups dominated in the power struggle both in Angola and Mozambique. The United States regarded political instability and armed conflict to be the greatest threats in Southern Africa. It feared that revolutionary change in the political systems of the region would be detrimental to American interests. American support for the liberation movements of Southern Africa was not substantial and the possible victory of the latter would have meant a shift in the balance of power at the expense of the United States.

Ramifications of a Racial Crisis

Apart from the American Cold War interest of expelling Soviet influence from the region, a serious concern of the United States was the potential political ramifications a race war in South Africa would have in American domestic politics. In the nineteen sixties, Americans, particularly Afro-Americans, were concerned largely with domestic issues and civil rights. But gradually the number of people who were aware of racial discrimination outside their country began to increase. Moreover, they were also becoming more concerned about American involvement in these issues. Trade unions, churches, universities and other groups were developing well organised strategies and programmes to exert influence on the United States government and multinationals operating in South Africa. Tilden J. LeMelle (1972, pp.98-100) observes this relation between domestic racial issues and foreign policy:

> The function of race across national boundaries has been perhaps the most obvious manifestation of an intraracial emanative relationship in international relations. . . . Expressions of transnational black racial ties are increasingly echoed across the Atlantic. . . . As far as transnational racial ties are concerned, it is instructive to note the pattern of linkage between domestic race relations and foreign policy.

The link between relations with South Africa and domestic American politics was something no administration could avoid. "Even though fine details may be lost or misperceived, the general tenor of U.S policy toward South Africa will be interpreted with reference to America's own racial issues" (Foltz, 1985, p.38). A study on United States-South African relations, involving in-depth interviews with more than eighty Americans who had power, influence or a specialist's knowledge in the field, stated that for Afro-Americans, policy towards South Africa was a litmus test of domestic racial attitudes. They regarded American relations with that country a mirror image of those attitudes (Baker, de St Jorre and O'Flaherty, 1979, pp.12-16).

The United States was also concerned about the attitudes of other Black African states over its policy towards South Africa. In the nineteen seventies the United States was strongly involved in political, economic and even military co-operation with some of them. The United States realised that it had to take into account the growing power of several Third World countries. One such country, which the United States had to reckon with was Nigeria. Nigeria was a major oil producing country, rapidly industrialising and in possession of an armed force of 250,000 men. Moreover, it had clearly emerged as a continental power with a strong policy on issues such as African economic ties with non-African countries. Nigeria also had strong views on the question of economic sanctions against South Africa. It impressed upon the United States that it was not interested in improved bilateral relations so long as the United States continued its support for the status quo in Southern Africa. The dependence of the United States on African, particularly Nigerian oil had significant implications for foreign policy.

The United States was concerned about the settlement of disputes in Southern Africa because among other reasons, continued racial conflict in the latter threatened its ability to progress on race relations at home and also because it affected the promotion of its interests in the rest of Africa.

South Africa: The Economic Locomotive of Africa

In economic terms, South Africa has one of the oldest and most developed economies in the whole of Africa. The country is large in size and population. Its Gross Domestic Product in 1960 was $2013 million, $5268 million in 1971 and $12785 million in 1977.[1] South Africa, in 1980 accounted for 20 per cent of the wealth of Africa; 40 per cent of its industrial productivity, including 80 per cent of the continent's steel production and 60 per cent of its electricity (Gann and Duignan, 1980, p.843; Stadler, 1987, pp.34-64). A statement of the South African Reserve Bank painted a very rosy picture of the economy thus:

> In a slow-growth or recession-minded world, the Republic of South Africa in 1980 can reasonably look forward to a growth rate of its real gross domestic product that may reach or exceed 5½ per cent. A healthy rate of expansion at this level would represent a further strengthening of the economic recovery that has been in evidence since late 1977 and gained considerable momentum in the second half of 1979.[2]

Although better known for its mining economy, manufacturing has developed into the most important sector of the South African economy. This expansion was mainly due to increased domestic demand and the policy of import substitution. Industrial output was dominated by engineering and metal products especially steel. Other major areas included automobile production and the chemical industry. In the agricultural sector there was an increase in overall production until the nineteen eighties. Maize, wheat, sugar cane, tobacco, deciduous fruits and vegetables constituted the most important produce. All these showed the strength of the South African economy which the United States had to take into account.

American Trade and Investment

Trade has been a dominant feature of United States-South African relations. While speaking of trade, it should be mentioned that in numerical terms United States trade with South Africa was only a small part of the former's world trade. However, South Africa was the United States' best customer in Africa. By the early seventies the United States had acquired a fairly substantial share of South Africa's foreign commerce. At the beginning of the seventies, the United States accounted for 17 per cent of South African imports and 13 per cent of its exports (*Southern Africa: Proposals for Americans*, 1971, p.18). On the other hand South Africa accounted for only 0.72 per cent of American imports and 1.3 per cent of exports. By 1980 these figures were 1.3 per cent and 1.1 per cent respectively. However, in monetary terms these figures were not insignificant amounting as they did to millions of dollars.

Table 2.1 **United States imports from South Africa compared with total US imports and imports from Africa** (In millions of US dollars)

	1970	1975	1977	1978	1979	1980
World	39952	96902	147671	171978	206256	244871
Africa	1113	8299	17121	16898	24382	34410
South Africa	290	840	1261	2259	2616	3321

Source: *Statistical Abstract of the United States 1984*, US Bureau of Census, Washington, DC., pp.834-837.

Table 2.2 United States exports to South Africa compared with total US exports and exports to Africa (In millions of US dollars)

	1970	1975	1977	1978	1979	1980
World	43224	107592	121212	143663	181816	220783
Africa	1580	4949	5546	5887	6299	9060
South Africa	563	1302	1054	1080	1413	2463

Source: *Statistical Abstract of the United States 1984,* US Bureau of Census, Washington, DC., pp.834-837.

In United States-South African trade, until 1975-76 the United States had a large surplus. In 1975 South Africa's trade deficit was $462 million. Referring to the American trade surplus, it was evident that it was beneficial to the United States balance of payments situation. The Report of a National Policy Panel of the United Nations Association of the United States of America (*Southern Africa: Proposals for Americans*, 1971, p.17) commented thus on a $275 million trade surplus in 1970:

> The significance of US trade with South Africa would appear to be more in terms of a US trade surplus. . . . When the US balance of payments is in heavy deficit and particularly when we are in a balance of trade deficit . . . it could be argued that this is an important figure.

By 1977 the situation changed. South Africa began having a trade surplus over the United States. During the period from 1978 to 1980 the rising price of gold was a factor which contributed to South Africa's better balance of payments position. However, by 1978 South Africa was still spending $500 million or more on American goods than Egypt, the United States' next best customer in Africa (Bertolin, 1978, p.32).

The nature of American investment in South Africa was more or less like that of trade. American investment in South Africa in the nineteen seventies accounted for between 1 per cent and 2 per cent of the total annual direct American investment overseas. In 1971 United States direct investment in South Africa was $860 million. For South Africa this represented 15 per cent of the total foreign investment in the country. By 1976 American direct investment in South Africa had reached at least $1.67 billion (Davis, 1977, p.17). Regarding returns on American investment, one would find that between the early fifties and late seventies, this ranged from 15 per cent to 20 per cent. This was much higher than returns world-wide as well as from the rest of Africa (Bertolin, 1978, p.25; Blashill, 1972, p.49).

Table 2.3 Direct and non-direct investment in South Africa
(in billions of dollars)

Direct investment	
EEC countries	6.9
Other European countries	0.9
North and South America	2.65
Africa	0.35
Rest of the world	0.23
Non-direct investment (includes bank loans, bond issues and portfolio investment by foreign investors)	
EEC countries	7.82
Other European countries	1.73
North and South America	3.59
Africa	0.46
Asia	0.46
International organisations	0.92

Source: *United States Policy Toward South Africa* (1980), Hearings before the Subcommittees on International Economic Policy and Trade; on Africa; and on International Organization of the Committee on Foreign Affairs, House of Representatives, 96th Congress, Second Session, Government Printing Office, Washington, DC., pp.653-657.

South Africa's growth into a highly developed economy led American multinational corporations to regard it as a profitable area for investment with a potential for further development. It was also regarded as one of the safest countries for foreign investment. Capital was not threatened by political vagaries, labour was cheap, the market was flourishing and the currency was hard and convertible. By 1980 the corporate stake consisted of 350 American companies with an aggregate direct investment of $2 billion (Jackson, 1982, p.226). The United States came second in the matter of investments in South Africa, after Britain.[3]

The American corporations involved in South Africa represented a cross section of the biggest business in the United States. The data of the United States Department of Commerce shows that roughly 50 per cent of the total American investment had gone into the manufacturing sector. Petroleum accounted for 20 per cent and mining 10 per cent and the remaining was shared by other sectors (*US Business Involvement in Southern Africa*, 1972, p.181). In a testimony before the House Subcommittee on Africa, Ann Seidman (1977, pp.23-25) stated that US based transnational corporations had put four out of every five dollars in manufacturing on the entire continent in South Africa. About 98 per cent of their investments in basic industry in Africa were in South Africa.

South Africa's automobile industry and the market for computers, as well as that of petroleum were dominated by American companies. During 1979, General Motors, Ford and Chrysler accounted for one-third of all motor vehicle sales in South Africa. These three Detroit giants had assets valued at $500 million and a total investment of $300 million in South Africa. In the nineteen seventies 70 per cent of the computer market was controlled by American manufacturers. For instance IBM itself controlled 25 per cent to 30 per cent of the market, making it South Africa's biggest supplier and servicer of computers. Three American oil companies: Caltex, Exxon and Mobil at one point controlled about 44 per cent of the petroleum market. In 1976 their sales exceeded $500 million, which was almost twice the sales of any other American corporation operating in South Africa. The combined assets of Caltex and Mobil were more than one-third of the total American investments in South Africa (Jackson, 1982, pp.263-268).

American banks had significant interests in South Africa. In times of political and economic crises they had come to the rescue of the apartheid economy. In the mid seventies Citibank, Morgan Guaranty Trust and the First National Bank of Chicago gave a $100 million loan to the South African government. The Citicorp International Bank took steps to provide a government owned parastatal (state corporation) with a loan of $100 million. There were also cases where British banks in which American banks had shares made loans to South Africa (Jackson, 1982, pp.269-270). By the second half of the seventies the total lending to South Africa by American banks reached its peak. Some American banks conscious of public pressure at home declared that they would not give loans to the South African government. At the same time they refused to deny loans to the private sector or for the purpose of financing trade. Timothy H. Smith points out that these banks had no operating social criteria which would negate one kind of loan to South Africa while allowing another (Smith, 1977, pp.12-14). Houser (1979, p.4) stated that trade related crediting, interbank loans or any underwriting of the South African economy had to be ended if genuine change had to take place. As long as the apartheid economy continued to function along the existing lines in ensuring stability and security, he added, White rule would be prolonged.

Table 2.4 Total lending of American banks to South Africa: 1975 to 1979

(From both United States offices and foreign branches. In millions of dollars of outstanding credits at the year end)

1975	1976	1977	1978	1979
1200	2200	2400	2000	1300

Source: *United States Policy Toward South Africa* (1980), Hearings before the Subcommittees on International Economic Policy and Trade; on Africa; and on International Organization of the Committee on Foreign Affairs, House of Representatives, 96th Congress, Second Session, Government Printing Office, Washington, DC., p.769.

Although American trade and investment were only between 1 per cent and 2 per cent of its total world-wide, this was not insignificant. The whole issue is not to be calculated in mere numerical terms, but seen as part of a significant vested interest in South Africa. American corporations had no desire to see even a small fraction of their overall investment being affected detrimentally as even this amounted to millions of dollars. American banking circles too feared the escalation of the racial crisis in South Africa and its possible economic impact as they had a stake in the economic and social stability there. Banks and corporations maintained the view that their interests would be safer under a White minority government. There was the possibility that political change could bring into power a government which would nationalise their assets. By the early nineteen seventies it came to be recognised that movements like the African National Congress advocated the total destruction of capitalism and big companies (Radu, 1987, p.73).

American corporations opposed disinvestment in South Africa, often justifying their presence and operations as essential to influence positive change in the country. The extent of economic ties between the two countries "provided an overwhelming political weight ... against the possible termination of the relationship as a form of leverage" (Bissel, 1982, p.75). Above all it was accepted in influential circles that disinvestment and withdrawal from any economic relationship with South Africa would be counterproductive. Many of the corporations had been operating there for a long time. Unilateral disinvestment particularly without the support of countries like Britain would be ineffective and would possibly result in other countries filling the resulting vacuum. This would ultimately result in the loss of whatever influence the United States already enjoyed. On the other hand by remaining in operation and by implementing better practices at the workplace, they could play a positive role. Once a corporation cut itself off from the economy it would both lessen its influence as well as negatively affect its renewed operations in future when the political situation had changed. Although the majority of the population lacked significant purchasing power, it was a potentially large market. Advocates of this approach therefore did not find disinvestment a feasible proposal in the long run.

South African Minerals

Southern Africa, particularly South Africa has been called the "Persian Gulf of Minerals". It has enormous reserves of several important minerals, on many of which the Western world relies for its supplies. By the seventies the United States depended on South Africa for many of these minerals. Although the United States is relatively rich in several minerals and had supplies enough at home for existing levels of production, the large scale growth and high levels of production resulted in demands that could not be met domestically. The United States thus became a significant importer of minerals and at times became critically dependent on foreign supplies. The United States Geological Survey identified twenty seven minerals as critical to industrial societies. South Africa has reserves and is an important producer of many of them. The United States was dependent on South Africa for several of these, mainly chromium, manganese, vanadium and platinum group metals.

Table 2.5 Principal minerals–US production as per cent of world production: 1970 to 1980

Mineral	1970	1975	1980
Manganese	-	-	-
Asbestos	3	2	2
Platinum group	-	-	-
Fluorspar	4	3	2
Chromium	-	-	-
Antimony	-	-	-
Titanium	23	22	14
Vanadium	26	20	13

Source: *Statistical Abstract of the United States 1984,* US Bureau of Census, Washington, DC., p.719.

It would be worth examining the important applications of these minerals, the degree of South African control over them, the alternative suppliers and the extent to which the United States was dependent on them.[4] Chromium occurs chiefly as chromite (ferrous chromite) in South Africa, Zimbabwe, the former Soviet Union, Philippines and Cuba. Of these reserves 95 per cent are concentrated in Southern Africa with 66.4 per cent in South Africa itself. The strategic value of chromium to the United States was not only because the United States lacked domestic reserves but also because American industries depended on it to make a wide variety of vital commodities including automobile and computer components. It is used in the production of stainless steel and in chemical industries. Chromium has been recognised as the final mineral for which supplies from one country are sufficiently high to cause potential problems. Problems could have arisen if the two southern African countries and the Soviet Union had withdrawn from the world market (Rees, 1985, p.169).

South Africa controls 37.2 per cent of the world's reserves and 20.9 per cent of the world's production of manganese. The United States has some deposits of only low grade ores. The principal producing countries are South Africa, the former Soviet Union, Gabon and India. Manganese is an essential ingredient in the large scale manufacture of wrought steel and there is no substitute for it. Of the world's vanadium reserves, 49.4 per cent are in South Africa, and it controls 42.3 per cent of its production too. Other vanadium deposits are in the former Soviet Union, Chile, Australia and Canada. Most vanadium is used in the production of iron and steel. It is also used in the production of ethylene-propylene rubber and the dye industry. It had been calculated in the late seventies that the United States' domestic resources were small and insufficient for more than a few years at annual consumption levels. Most of the world's platinum comes from South Africa and the erstwhile Soviet Union. South Africa itself has about 73.2 per cent of the world's reserves of platinum group metals. Of the American imports, about 67 per cent used to come from South Africa. The unique properties of platinum group metals make them useful for many applications in industry as catalysts in the production of high octane gasoline, acids, drugs and chemicals. They are also used in the automobile industry, glass industry, the making of laboratory equipment and synthetic fibres as well as for cancer therapy.

Table 2.6 Net US imports of selected minerals as per cent of apparent consumption: 1970 to 1980

Mineral	1970	1978	1979	1980	Rank of foreign sources 1978-1981
Manganese	95	97	98	98	Gabon, South Africa, Australia
Asbestos	83	85	83	78	Canada, South Africa
Platinum group	78	90	89	88	South Africa, USSR, UK
Chromium	89	91	90	91	South Africa, USSR, Philippines
Titanium	24	41	39	32	Australia, Canada, South Africa
Vanadium	21	36	28	35	South Africa, Chile, Canada

Note: Figures based on net imports which equal the difference between imports and exports plus or minus government stockpile and industry stock changes.

Source: *Statistical Abstract of the United States 1984,* US Bureau of Census, Washington, DC., p.721.

South Africa is the world's leading producer of gold. A little more than half of the world's reserves of gold are in South Africa. In the late seventies it produced more than six times that of the Soviet Union, the next largest producer. South Africa produced 75 per cent of the western world's supply of newly mined gold and the United States depended on it for 45 per cent of its gold needs. The monetary aspects of gold have long dominated commercial interest in the metal. Disruption of the supply would have its impact on world gold sales and international economic stability. However, supplies were not crucial to the world from a strategic or industrial standpoint. United States production, government stockpiles and holdings of other developed countries were sufficient to meet the needs for some time. In addition to these, the United States was also importing from South Africa asbestos, titanium, diamonds, antimony and uranium.

This was the kind of dependence the United States had on South African minerals. Not only was disruption in the supply of vital minerals critical, such disruption could not be predicted or controlled. As a consequence, prices could go up and physical shortages could have adverse economic and political consequences on the countries dependent on them. In the wake of the oil crisis of 1973 and the emergence of the Organisation of Petroleum Exporting Countries (OPEC) such a scenario was no longer regarded impossible. The same conditions could take place in the case of non-fuel minerals and metals elsewhere in the world, particularly South Africa.

The excessive reliance of the United States on South Africa for non-fuel minerals caused concern in many quarters. Congressmen like Representative James Santini, Chairman of the House Mines and Mining Subcommittee, after a fact finding trip to Southern Africa in 1980 warned of this dependence. His report stated that no issue facing the United States in the future posed as much risk and danger as the dependence on foreign sources for strategic and critical minerals (Jackson, 1982, p.182).

For the United States the significance of the problem was not merely because of South Africa's position as the repository of these minerals, but was also due to the fact that in most cases the alternative suppliers were either the Soviet Union or its allies. Rees (1985, p.168) illustrates the unusual case regarding platinum group metals, where South Africa and the Soviet Union, in an "unholy alliance" colluded over the supply and price, as they did in the case of gold and diamonds. Secondly, it had not been a problem of the United States alone. Its allies in Western Europe and Japan had been more dependent on South Africa. The European Community was dependent on it for 49 per cent of its chromium, 41 per cent of manganese, 18 per cent of platinum group metals and to a lesser degree for vanadium. Japan's dependence was even higher (Bowman, 1982, p.170).

All these factors taken together, i.e., South Africa's overall production, the West's dependence on it and the position of the Soviet Union and its allies as primary alternative suppliers strengthened South Africa's standing in the American viewpoint.

Geographic and Strategic Importance

No less important were South Africa's geographic location and strategic importance. Its position at the southern tip of the African continent is sometimes regarded to be as important as its mineral wealth. For several centuries the Cape of Good Hope had been of strategic importance to western shipping. South Africa's waterways connect the great oceans. Yet, the United States had not recognised Africa's strategic importance for a long time. In the introduction to his article entitled "United States Military and Strategic Interests in Africa", William J. Foltz (1986, p.43) states:

> [T]he title of this paper is a sad sign of the times in which we live. Throughout almost all of US history, America's military and strategic interests in Africa would scarcely have merited a paragraph in anything other than an ambitious naval officer's dream book.

In the nineteen seventies, the region from the Horn of Africa to Southern Africa became important for both superpowers. In the context of oceanic shipping it was argued that the southern tip of Africa was of great strategic significance because much of the oil that was being shipped to the West went around the Cape. Modern shipping does not require intermediate ports of call for refuelling, but the forces of nature have not been fully controlled by modern technology. In the southern hemisphere the fierce Westerly winds and the turbulent seas of the Roaring Forties between the southern tip of Africa and Antarctica make it necessary for marine vessels to keep close to the South African coastline.

The Cape sea route is one of the world's busiest sea lanes. It is also the main access route to the West for its oil tankers coming from the Persian Gulf. These ships transported 70 per cent of West Europe's strategic minerals, 25 per cent of its food supply; 65 per cent of West Europe's and 28 per cent of the United States oil imports around the Cape (Jackson, 1982, p.227; Foltz, 1985, p.33). Although the United States was in 1979 the world's single largest producer of oil, at about 10.3 million barrels a day, it was at the same time the world's single largest consumer also, at about 19 million barrels a day (Ramazani, 1983, p.9). The United States dependence on oil imports was thus about half of its consumption and both were increasing annually. Moreover, even a shortfall of 5 per cent would have been disruptive to the American economy (Shepherd, 1983, p.228). Stookey (1975, p.57) highlights this point thus:

> Most Americans were shocked to learn in October 1973 that imports of Arab oil represented the margin between opulent life and austerity. Few realized that the United States was then importing a million barrels per day of Arab crude and an additional million barrels of products refined from oil originating in Arab states; this represented 14% of the American oil supply and 7% of all energy consumed.

As statistics show, by the end of the nineteen seventies the Cape sea route had served 27,000 ships annually. Every month about 2,300 ships including 600 oil tankers used the route. Half of these ships called on South African ports annually while the rest circumnavigated the Cape without stopping (Bowman, 1982, p.161). In the context of discussing the Cape route and its importance, the significance or rather limitations of the Suez Canal have to be examined. It is true that the Suez Canal reduces the distance from West Asia to the West considerably.[5] But three factors have contributed to the diminution of the utility of the Canal to the United States. Firstly, the conflicts in West Asia particularly the Arab-Israeli wars had made the Suez Canal part of an international trouble spot. In 1956, 1967 and 1973 the Canal had to be closed because of the war. Although the Canal was closed, with excess tanker capacity available, the additional time factor involved in the Cape route was insignificant (Venn, 1986, p.132). Secondly, the physical dimensions of the Suez Canal prevent navigation of certain vessels. Despite the enlargement of the Canal between 1975 and 1980, only ships up to the 53 foot draft can be accommodated. The Canal is currently open only to oil tankers of the capacity of 110,000 dead weight tons (dwt) empty and 70,000 dwt fully loaded (Du Jonchay, 1978, p.62). Ultra Large Crude Carriers (ULCC) cannot navigate through it on account of their size, and a significant amount of oil is transported to the West in such supertankers. The third factor against the Suez route is regarding the costs involved. While considering the tolls levied at the Suez for a ship travelling both ways, the Cape route is less expensive. In the late seventies it added roughly $2 to the cost of a metric tonne of crude oil shipped on a medium sized vessel used in both directions on the Suez route. It penalised such a ship about $1 to the tonne, relative to a VLCC (Very Large Crude Carrier) going around the Cape. These reasons made the Cape sea route an alternative to the Suez route and attractive to the West (Du Jonchay, 1978, p.10; *Southern Africa: The Escalation of Conflict*, 1976, p.52).

Defence Interests

The United States also had defence interests in South Africa. In the past it had made use of several South African facilities. Of these the most important were those offered at the naval base of Simonstown, near Cape Town. It was for several years used by Britain, and under the 1955 naval co-operation agreement it had signed with South Africa, the United States, as an ally of the former, acquired guaranteed access to the naval and air facilities in times of war, notwithstanding South Africa's status as a belligerent or not.[6] The naval base served as one of the main bases for naval communication. It was one of the most modern and sophisticated ones in the southern hemisphere, being fully equipped by western experts, containing naval repair wharves and a training centre for submarines. South African naval facilities had also been available at Saldanha Bay and Walvis Bay on the Atlantic coast and at Richards Bay and Durban on the Indian Ocean. There were also operational airfields throughout South Africa from which strike aircraft could operate.

The growing importance of the Indian Ocean in the nineteen seventies also contributed to South Africa's significance. It was widely recognised that the Indian Ocean offered to the power which dominated it, potential control over the rimlands of Africa, West Asia and the Indian subcontinent, and that this could be accomplished only through a maritime strategy (Roherty, 1985, p.279). For the United States the Cape of Good Hope was the principal maritime entry point to the Indian Ocean. It was roughly at mid transit between the important American base at Norfolk, Virginia and the Persian Gulf. South Africa could provide a main base without parallel, as well as other infrastructure and facilities. The South African Navy which was no longer in partnership with the Royal Navy after 1974 had realised that it could not maintain a blue water role and wanted to dramatise the issue for the United States.[7] By 1979, events in Iran and Afghanistan led the

United States to consider the specifics of naval collaboration with South Africa.

Highly sophisticated intelligence and communication facilities were available to the United States at Silvermine, ten kilometres north of Simonstown. There was a military radar surveillance installation at Silvermine which could monitor any aerial movement or shipping throughout the southern oceans. The centrepiece of South Africa's activities had been Project Advokaat, with its main centre at Silvermine and substations in Durban and Walvis Bay. In addition, the electronic equipment there could provide in a matter of seconds, information about ships in the area to conflict monitoring centres in the United States and Britain. The installation could also do the surveillance of over fifty countries. Apart from that, the statistics of around 20,000 war and merchant ships of eighty five countries were computerised at Silvermine (*The White House and the Black Continent*, 1984, p.64). This network probably extended to the Bay of Bengal (Kapur, 1983, p.141). At one time the communications centre was linked to the North Atlantic Treaty Organisation's Identification Friend or Foe (IFF) system and provided the United States Navy at its Puerto Rico base with full intelligence on constant surveillance of Soviet and other shipping (Bowman, 1982, p.175). There also had been some circumspect co-operation between some western countries and South Africa. The information collected at the major signals intelligence facility established in 1973 with the assistance of the National Security Agency and Government Communication Headquarters of South Africa, was then passed on to the United States, Britain and some countries of the Commonwealth (Richelson and Ball, 1985, p.173). The United States had a strategic interest in access to intelligence in the region and the surrounding oceans. The Indian Ocean had by the nineteen seventies become a scene of American activity particularly for nuclear missile carrying submarines. In connection with these activities the United States required the assistance of South Africa.

On the other hand those who discounted South Africa's strategic significance argued that the importance of its facilities was only in the event of hostilities. They also regarded the facilities to be somewhat antiquated. Another argument was that the United States had its own technical intelligence gathering capacity and that there had been an increasing redundancy of far-flung and vulnerable ground stations (Berridge, 1990, p.211).

One could not predict the occurrence of hostilities. But in the event of a crisis, the United States would have had to use South Africa's facilities. In such a situation the fact that these facilities were antiquated could only have been of less importance. Facilities like that of Silvermine were always of significance as a back up service. In that part of the world they were perhaps the only available facilities and the United States would have no option but to make use of them. It had not been possible for the West to acquire direct control of bases along the oil route. At the same time the West had an overriding interest in preventing the Soviet Union from acquiring one. Since the late nineteen fifties the Soviet Union had wanted to obtain air and naval access in Southern Africa to counter United States strategic forces, to monitor American military activity and provide assistance to friendly regimes in the region. This was one of the reasons why, despite the limited facilities South Africa could offer, several circles in the United States sought to highlight their importance and the need to maintain access to them. Officials in the Pentagon admitted that Southern Africa, particularly South Africa, was an area which, while not critical, nevertheless had importance for American strategic interests because it was an area adjacent to the sea lanes of communication between the South Atlantic and the Indian Ocean. They also found in South Africa the only harbours south of the Sahara which had facilities capable of handling major vessels. Furthermore, its geographical location had been particularly well suited for facilities in support of American missile and space programmes (*US Business Involvement in Southern Africa*, 1972, p.92).

South Africa also was prepared to carry out regional tasks on behalf of the West and constantly sought greater military co-operation with the United States. It vigorously promoted seaward defence and occasionally put out feelers on the formation of a South Atlantic Treaty Organisation. As early as 1970 the South African government had proposed the conclusion of a treaty by which it could become an associate member of the NATO (*The White House and the Black Continent*, 1984, pp.64-65). In the past it had shown willingness to put its armed forces under NATO command, deploy a NATO contingent on its territory and allow it the use of Simonstown and other facilities. An official South African government publication gave the reasons why the West needed South Africa. It mentioned the importance of the Cape sea lanes and the Communist threat to them. It stated that the security of these sea lanes, the Southern Atlantic and the Indian Ocean were not only for the safety of South Africa but other countries as well. It also urged individual western countries to make their contribution to safeguarding the sea lanes.[8] The focus of South Africa's strategic thinking, shared by many in the United States, was the American-Soviet rivalry in the Southern hemisphere. The denial of continental lodging to the Soviet Union was fundamental to the long term security interests of South Africa. Consequently, alignment with the United States was a dominant issue in any strategic design that it had.

The increasing need for United States and NATO military co-operation with South Africa was clearly expressed in the mid seventies in the background of the happenings in Angola and Mozambique, particularly by people like former US Admiral John McCain. He believed that these developments and the importance of Diego Garcia meant that the United States needed access to South African naval facilities (Johnson, 1975, p.10). Despite the differing views regarding the level of the need for military co-operation with South Africa, it was recognised that the country had developed into a strong regional military power. From \$110.5 million in 1969-70, South Africa's defence expenditure increased rapidly to \$754.8 million in 1979-80.[9] The arms embargoes of 1963 and 1977 had a significant impact on South Africa by forcing it to manufacture its own weapons instead of relying on imports. The boycott had paradoxically led South Africa to attain self-sufficiency in arms production with the support of western countries. In 1968 it established the Armaments Development and Production Corporation (ARMSCOR) which had grown into one of the largest industrial undertakings in South Africa and by 1983 was the world's tenth largest arms producer. ARMSCOR was in a position to supply virtually all the country's defence end products including aircraft, ordnance, small arms, artillery, electro-optical systems and missiles (Todd, 1988, p.259). The only area in which it was deficient was offensive air and sea strike power (Jenkins, 1980, p.24). In addition to being an arms producer South Africa became an arms exporter. From 1970 to 1979 the White Rhodesian regime obtained the bulk of South Africa's arms exports. Grundy (1986, p.48) wrote that if ARMSCOR developed an export capacity, then business input into foreign policy decisions would expand.

Nuclear and Space Co-operation

The United States and South Africa also had co-operation in nuclear and space programmes. In the nuclear sphere the two countries had been co-operating on an energy generating programme and in research activities since 1950. South Africa possessed large reserves of uranium ore in which the United States was interested. This eventually led to technological co-operation in the form of training South African nuclear scientists in the United States and the installation of a research reactor in South Africa with American assistance. Walters (1976, p.26) maintains that there existed a situation where the American trade in nuclear materials with South Africa had beneath it a rationale rooted in international economic competition for an important market. At the same time this trade was also well integrated with the United States military and strategic objectives. But over the years the United States was becoming concerned about South Africa's alleged activities in the nuclear weapons programme. Despite American insistence, South Africa refused to sign the Nuclear Nonproliferation Treaty. South Africa was interested in nuclear weapons to compensate for its political isolation, to impress its allies and opponents alike, and also to threaten neighbouring Black states. The nuclear dimension in United States-South African relations thus turned out to be a rallying point for both antiapartheid and anti-nuclear forces. Although the United States stopped exports of enriched uranium to South Africa in 1975, the latter could overcome this impediment by obtaining the necessary fuel from its own enrichment facility or an alternative supplier. In 1977 there were reports of a nuclear weapons site in the Kalahari desert. In 1979 an American VELA surveillance satellite detected a flash over the South Atlantic near South Africa. Many observers claimed that it had been a secret nuclear test, possibly conducted jointly by South Africa and Israel. But the United States government concluded that it was not a nuclear explosion conducted by South Africa (Patterson, 1984, p.139). By then there was a general consensus among South Africa watchers that it was a nuclear power–if not already one, it was on the threshold of being so.[10]

There was also co-operation in the field of space research between the United States and South Africa. Often it is difficult to separate activities in this sphere with those connected with defence. Since 1952 the United States had an arrangement for the exchange of South African unclassified maps and aeronautical charts of Southern Africa. The United States also had several projects including the collection of geodetic information in Southern Africa, the collection of magnetic information and also of data from United States navigation satellites (*US Business Involvement in Southern Africa*, 1972, p.94). Following the signing in 1961 of a bilateral agreement, agencies designated by both governments operated the Deep Space Instrumentation Facility, the Space Tracking and Data Acquisition Network and an Optical Tracking Station in South Africa. The National Aeronautics and Space Administration (NASA) maintained that because of its geographic position, the location of the station in South Africa was eminently desirable (*The Faces of Africa*, 1972, pp.159-160). The United States Air Force Tracking Station in South Africa also played a key role in American missile and space development programmes. NASA tracking facilities in South Africa were considered helpful for the United States but not essential.[11] Alternative facilities could be developed in the Malagasy Republic off the coast of Africa and also in other areas where conditions were suitable. On the other hand, the Department of State maintained that removal of the NASA tracking station would harm the United States space programme without leading to constructive consequences in South Africa's racial or other relations.[12]

Having observed South Africa's economic situation, mineral resources, strategic location, defence potential, possession of advanced equipment and sophisticated facilities, strategists wanted the United States to accept it as a useful western ally. They believed that this would be beneficial in times of hostilities. The favourable attitude of the United States towards South Africa was not only due to its enormous mineral wealth but was also because of political considerations. Washington regarded Pretoria as a reliable economic and military ally in times of crises, when the supply of strategic minerals could be affected (*US Economic Expansion: Asia and Africa*, 1986, p.78).

Some observers state that the importance of the Cape route was often overstated by South Africa and its friends. For them there was no threat of a total onslaught on South Africa by the Soviet Union. It was true that the Soviets were supporting some of the liberation movements in Southern Africa and also supplying some Black states with weapons. But these were not signs of developing any infrastructure or plan that would launch a take-over of South Africa. There has been much contention among strategists on the character and quality of the Soviet threat. On the other hand it was argued that strategists were not planning for the existing state of affairs but were looking at the future possibilities and how options could be covered. As Leach (1987, p.276) observed:

> Another Middle East War could render the Cape route of vital importance once again, a sudden heightening of tension in Europe for whatever reason could spill over into other areas of the world where the superpowers are outfacing each other.

Apart from the need for military-strategic relations with the United States, South Africa needed close ties with the former for economic, psychological and diplomatic reasons. American investment formed a sizeable part of the South African economy and the United States was South Africa's best customer for minerals and raw materials. Strategic ties with the United States paid dividends in the form of status in the region and deterrence against attacks from Communist powers, neighbouring Black states or liberation movements. Equally important was the American support at the diplomatic level, particularly at the United Nations in the form of the veto.

By the early nineteen seventies the debate in the United States regarding South Africa and its importance was gaining ground. By the end of the decade this debate grew intense. On the one hand there was a strong demand in several circles that punitive action be taken against South Africa for pursuing apartheid. On the other hand the advocates of South Africa's importance believed that such measures would only alienate the country, push it into the Communist embrace and detrimentally affect the majority Blacks of that country. They highlighted the need for the United States to encourage regionally dominant anti-Communist states which were strongly committed to spending their own resources for their defence. The ultimate question was whether the United States had to continue its profitable relations with South Africa and turn a Nelson's eye on apartheid or end those relations and champion the cause of the oppressed in South Africa.

Notes

1. The figures are from L. H. Gann and Peter Duignan (1981), *Why South Africa Will Survive,* Croom Helm, London, p.153. The figures have been converted from Rand to dollar at 1985 rates.
2. "Recent Developments in the South African Economy", A Statement by the South African Reserve Bank, in *The Economist* (London), June 21, 1980, pp. 16-17.
3. Britain had the closest economic ties with South Africa for historical reasons. About 10 per cent of its world-wide foreign direct investment had been in South Africa. In formulating its policies towards South Africa, the United States has traditionally been concerned with the economic effects these policies might have on Britain. This concern had been largely motivated by fear of the effect on the dollar of a weakened position for the pound sterling, one of the world's most important reserve currencies.
4. The statistics regarding South African reserves, production and American import of minerals from South Africa are from *South Africa: Time Running Out* (1981), University of California Press, Berkeley.
5. The distance from New York to Ras Tanura in Saudi Arabia by the Cape route is 19,000 km and by the Suez route is 13,300. The saving is about 30 per cent.
6. In 1968 South Africa repudiated the agreement but made it clear that the West could use it if the former deemed it in its interests to make it available.

7. Some writers highlighted the importance of South Africa for the security and prosperity of the free world. See Robert J. Hanks (1983), *Southern Africa and Western Security*, Institute for Foreign Policy Analysis, Cambridge, MA.
8. "Why the West needs South Africa", reprinted from an official South African Government publication, in *Africa Report* (New York), vol. 20(1), January-February 1975, p.20.
9. The figures are from Richard E. Bissel (1982), *South Africa and the United States: The Erosion of an Influence Relationship*, Praeger, New York, p. 63. The figures have been converted from Rand to dollar at 1985 rates.
10. In early 1993 the South African President F. W. de Klerk disclosed that his country had produced six Hiroshima size atomic weapons during the days of high apartheid but had destroyed the arsenal in 1989.
11. NASA ended its co-operation with South Africa with regard to the tracking stations in 1975.
12. Department of State's reply to Chairman Digg's Action Manifesto dated February 18, 1972, *The Faces of Africa: Diversity and Progress; Repression and Struggle, Report of Special Study Missions to Africa* (1972), House Committee on Foreign Affairs, 92nd Congress, Second Session, Government Printing Office, Washington, DC., pp.113-114.

3 The United States and South Africa Until 1969: An Overview

To the seventeenth century North American colonists, Southern Africa was a familiar region despite being separated by a vast expanse of the waters of the Atlantic. Although Southern Africa was not particularly known for slaves, there are evidences of Africans having been brought to the Americas from the eastern shores of Africa by ships sailing around the Cape of Good Hope. By the time the United States had come into existence, Southern Africa's importance as the gateway to the Indian Ocean had increased, particularly with the bustling commercial activity of the new nation.[1] Cape Town had become an essential port of call in the American maritime itinerary and trading ships were a familiar sight there. It was natural that the surrounding land and its produce evoked interest in the Americans. In *Moby Dick*, Herman Melville wrote that the Cape of Good Hope and all the watery region about there was "much like some noted four corners of a great highway" where one would "meet more travellers than in any other part". In the eighteen fifties when he wrote his classic, American whaling ships used to sail to Southern African waters from the New England ports of Nantucket, Newport and New Bedford.

American missionaries, miners and prospectors also made their presence felt in the area that is today known as South Africa. The American Board of Commissioners for Foreign Missions (ABCFM) and the American Methodist Episcopal Church (AME) were some of those active in spreading the gospel. Between 1850 and 1870 the discovery in South Africa, first of gold and later of diamonds brought many American miners and prospecters into the country. Appolon Davidson (1984, p.59), a biographer of Cecil Rhodes, describes these men as being full of radiant hope and who believed in their stars and their own strength.

The United States during this period adhered to isolationism, a national policy of avoiding entanglement in foreign affairs. But this did not preclude American commercial activity around the globe. Africa, excluding Liberia and South Africa, did not figure much in the American scheme of things. Although it sent representatives to the Berlin Conference of 1884-85, convened for the partition of Africa, the United States declared that it could not "join in the responsible political engagements in so remote and undefined a region as that of the Congo Basin" (Ferrel, 1975, p.755). If there was any American policy towards Africa, it was influenced by the European colonial powers especially Britain. However, for commercial reasons the United States had already established its first consulate in Cape Town in 1799, to be followed by others in Johannesburg, Pretoria and Durban in 1891, 1898 and 1906 respectively (Bissel, 1982, p.5).

One particular event that evoked some American interest in South Africa was the Boer War of 1899-1902 between the British and the Boers. Although the American leadership sympathised with Britain, the United States maintained neutrality, lest it alienate a large number of Dutch and Irish immigrants who supported the Boer cause. The American sympathies and support for Britain have been attributed to racial, economic and humanitarian considerations. The United States considered Britain a force for progress in South Africa. Moreover, it believed that Britain would protect and foster the non-political objectives of the United States in South Africa (Noer, 1978).

The Inter-War Period

Following World War I, South Africa joined the League of Nations which was very much a creation of Jan Christian Smuts as that of Woodrow Wilson. Smuts' proposals on the League of Nations, particularly the nature and composition of the Council and the Mandate system, influenced Wilson to a great extent. Under the Mandate system, instituted to govern the colonies of defeated powers, South Africa received South West Africa (Namibia), the independence of which was a prominent issue until 1990 and in which the United States had a major role to play. It was during World War I that the United States made an entry into the South African economy in a significant manner. The penetration of American capital was instrumental in offsetting the economic instability associated with the war and resulted in the acquisition by the mining industry of sufficient capital to start new ventures. One such example was the Anglo-American Corporation established in 1917 by the Oppenheimers with assistance from J. P. Morgan of the United States.

As regards diplomatic relations between the United States and South Africa, the interwar period was of significance. South Africa opened a diplomatic mission in the United States in 1929 and its first press and public relations officer to that country was appointed in 1942. By 1938 the United States had realised the growing interest it had in Africa particularly South Africa so much so that it created a desk in the Department of State to deal exclusively with affairs of the continent. However, on the international scene, the United States withdrew into its cocoon of isolationism, whereas South Africa continued to be an active member of the community of nations.

The Post-War Period

After World War II, American capital found its way into more areas of the South African economy like petroleum, automobiles, shipping, refrigeration, tyres, textiles and hosiery. What facilitated its smooth entry were the political and economic conditions prevailing in South Africa at that time. Simultaneously, particularly after 1948, when South Africa strengthened its racial apparatus, several steps were taken to improve relations with the United States. These included the strengthening of the embassy in Washington and the establishment of new consular missions in various parts of the United States, bringing the total to nine, which was not an insignificant number. The United States also reciprocated with the upgradation of its consulate in Pretoria to an embassy in 1949.

By 1950, apartheid had acquired international notoriety and had become a burning issue at the United Nations. The United States was until 1960, in the words of Coker (1986, p.4), "a dispassionate, if not disinterested observer" of South African affairs. During this period it was reluctant to make a choice between its economic interests and moral responsibilities. In the 1952 United Nations debate, the United States took a "middle of the road" position, wishing to avoid both "excess of zeal and timid legalism" in dealing with the question (Vandenbosch, 1970, p.235). On the one hand, it questioned the rationality of apartheid and criticised it for not being in conformity with the generally accepted notions of the obligations of the Charter of the United Nations, while on the other, it continued to emphasise the limitations of the world body in intervening in matters strictly within the domestic jurisdiction of states. To the United States, proclaiming standards was one thing, imposing them was another. The American middle of the road position was puzzling both to adversaries of apartheid as well as the South Africans themselves. John Gunther (1955, p.544), traveller and writer, on a visit to South Africa asked a cabinet minister what he thought of American policy towards Africa in general and South Africa in particular. The response of the minister was that it was impossible to give an answer because nobody in his country had been able to figure out what American policy was. South African ministers and officials often complained that they were confused about deciding which of the several American voices represented United States policy.

In 1959, the United Nations General Assembly condemned South Africa's racist policies as a threat to international harmony, much beyond being a domestic matter. The United States joined the other sixty one nations voting for the motion to this effect. On the occasion the American delegate declared that "apartheid was a violation of human rights buttressed and sanctified by law" (Troup, 1972, p.358). For many it represented a change from the earlier American position. But not so for Eric Louw, the South African Foreign Minister, who attributed it to the pressures operating in the United States, whose delegation was led by a prominent labour leader known for his anti-South African stance. In essence, Louw was stating that whatever was said in public, the United States would not pursue policies that were antagonistic to South Africa (Barber, 1973, p.66).

The late nineteen fifties and early sixties witnessed the turmoil of independence movements in Africa. The dedication of the United States to peaceful and gradual change came to be questioned increasingly. The Eisenhower administration was caught in the obsession with Communism which debilitated its ability to comprehend the emerging African situation. The Sharpville shootings in South Africa in which about seventy Blacks were killed, was a clear message to the United States that its national interest would be served only by distancing itself from the White minority regime. The prevalent attitude among American policymakers was that in contrast to regions like West Asia, there were no exigent crises to deal with in Africa. African issues including that of apartheid were to them, not of the proportion of the Suez crisis of 1956 or even the other Arab-Israeli wars (Ferrel, 1975, p.756).

The New Frontier and Apartheid

With John F. Kennedy's assumption of the presidency, it was widely believed that a re-examination of American policy towards South Africa would be made. Africa had figured in his political career and he perceived anticolonialism as a useful weapon in the Cold War, which even as an influence, would in course of time weaken the attraction of Communism in the Third World. Kennedy was vociferous and critical of American support to France on the Algerian issue. He later became the chairman of the Subcommittee on Africa of the Senate Foreign Relations Committee. He thought that the American liberal concept of civil rights could be propagated in Africa not only through anticolonialism but also through foreign aid. Kennedy's selection of senior officials and advisers, many of them supporters of the civil rights campaign at home, sent the message that he meant business as far as apartheid was concerned. Men like Adlai Stevenson and G. Mennen Williams along with the ambassadors to Africa were strongly pro-African or liberal American intellectuals.[2] Of the several appointments made, that of G. Mennen Williams as Assistant Secretary of State for African Affairs was perhaps the most important in this context.

But the Kennedy administration could not bring any substantial change in American policy. While embarking on the ritual condemnation of apartheid, it also attempted to convince South Africa through diplomatic channels of the futility of its policy. But Washington was not only disinclined to participate in coercive measures designed to do away with apartheid but also co-operated with South Africa on matters of strategic importance. A critic of American policy remarked that as long as South Africa continued with apartheid, the United States could not justify any kind of economic aid even if it was "clothed in the rationalization of military defence" (*The United States in the United Nations, 1960: A Turning Point*, 1961, p.12). Efforts by the international community to impose sanctions on South Africa were opposed by American delegates on the ground that they would not accomplish the purpose. Such measures, they believed, would create internal problems in South Africa and would detrimentally affect the victims of apartheid themselves (Plimpton, 1961, p.602).

The United States continued to co-operate with South Africa on military and strategic matters. American naval ships continued to call on South African ports. At the same time an agreement was announced for the establishment of a United States military space tracking station in South Africa. This was meant to reciprocate the American sale of arms to South Africa for use against Communist aggression. A similar policy was being followed by the United States towards Portugal and its Southern African colonies. In this case the strategic position and facilities of the Azores was the determining factor.

In 1960 and 1961 at the sessions of the United Nations General Assembly, the African countries introduced resolutions demanding political and economic sanctions against South Africa. But their proposals did not obtain the required two-thirds majority. In the autumn of 1962 African states brought a new resolution calling on members of the United Nations to sever their political and economic relations with South Africa. They also requested the Security Council to consider expelling South Africa from the world body if it did not bring about reforms. Kennedy did not approve of the resolution. He felt that sanctions would not work if South Africa's major trading partners refused to adhere to them (Schlesinger, 1965, p.535). Ambassador Plimpton (1962, p.794) stated that apartheid could not be ended by the contraction of relations between South Africans and the rest of the world, but by the enlargement of those relationships and the continued exposure of the South African government to world opinion. Although the resolution was opposed by the United States, the General Assembly passed it with a large majority.

By now it was clear that the United States was deliberately trying to distract international attention from its lucrative economic and strategic ties with South Africa. The administration was aware that this posture was having a negative impact on American standing in the eyes of Third World nations. To rectify this it attempted at toughening the American position on apartheid. African leaders made it clear to the United States that it could no longer cling on to mere verbal condemnation, but had to go beyond. One doubt that the administration expressed was whether the provisions of Chapter VII of the United Nations Charter would apply to the South African case. Schlesinger (1965, p.535) claims that this argument as well as the faith Africans had in Kennedy convinced them of the American stand on the issue.

The great hopes placed by Africans on Kennedy, Williams and the New Frontier were eroding, for whatever officials of the administration said appeared to be mere public relations exercises. Patrick Duncan, a prominent White South African antiapartheid politician wrote that until then American policy in Africa had tried to avoid making choices by trying to satisfy both colonial powers and the new African nations. Such a policy, he considered wise, if there was either a continuing dialogue between contending parties or when political movement was generally in the desired direction, or when either side was subject to persuasion. Whereas, as Duncan observed, in the case of South Africa, none of these conditions applied (Duncan, 1963, p.42).

Mennen Williams in a memorandum stated that action had to accompany disapproval and the area where this could be demonstrated was in the case of arms sales. The existing agreement with South Africa for the sale of arms in return for the tracking station stood as an obstacle. Neither would a full arms embargo attain the level of sanctions demanded by the majority of the members of the United Nations. The administration was in a dilemma. It was planning a total arms embargo while the African states desired nothing less than a full economic embargo. This was the situation from which the United States was seeking to escape. The opportunity arrived in August 1963 when the Security Council was debating a resolution calling for a ban on all arms sales to South Africa. The American ambassador, Adlai Stevenson announced that the United States was bringing to an end the sale of all military equipment to the Government of South Africa by the end of the calendar year "in order further to contribute to a peaceful solution and to avoid any steps which might at this point directly contribute to international friction" in Southern Africa. He said that there were existing contracts, which provided for the supply of limited quantities of strategic equipment for defence against external threats, which had to be honoured. Stevenson, however, also stated that given its world-wide responsibilities, the United States would in future have the right to interpret the policy in the light of requirements for guaranteeing the maintenance of international peace and security (Stevenson, 1963, pp.333-337).

What did the United States intend by the sudden announcement of ceasing supplies of arms to South Africa? The United States had come to realise that its existing policy was being increasingly questioned and that there was a possibility of the resolution being adopted. As Waldemar Nielsen (1969, p.296) suggests, the United States did so either to avoid the appearance of complying with a UN action, or to gain credit for the initiative, or to create a smokescreen behind which to fulfil previous military commitments. The United States eventually voted for the resolution which called on all states "to cease forthwith the sale and shipment of arms, ammunition and all types of military vehicles to South Africa". It has to be reiterated that it was a voluntary arms embargo, not a mandatory one. Charles Yost, Stevenson's deputy, emphasised that in the American view, the situation in South Africa did not warrant mandatory sanctions (Yost, 1963, pp.333-337). In retrospect, the American strategy was to make a clear demarcation around its position while simultaneously yielding in some measure to Third World pressure. "The resulting posture resembled one of straddling the fence, with an ear to the ground, an eye to the future, and a finger in the dyke" (Nielsen, 1969, p.297).

Towards the end of the Kennedy administration, the situation in South Africa had not improved in the least. Appeals to South Africa from the world community fell on deaf ears. The United States remained opposed to mandatory sanctions and refused to accept the view that South African issues were threats to peace within the definitions and scope provided in the UN Charter. On the other hand the United States seemed keen to dissociate from South African leaders. For instance the only high level contact from 1958 to 1966 was in 1962, between Dean Rusk , the Secretary of State and Eric Louw, the South African Foreign Minister (Geldenhuys, 1984, p.18). In this regard Kennedy was different from his predecessors and displayed a pro-nationalist disposition towards African countries. But, in the words of David Burner (1988, p.84), "his penchant was for making decisions at the margin, committing little and leaving room for escape".

The Great Society and Apartheid

During the first months of the Johnson administration, despite the increasing preoccupation with Vietnam, policy towards South Africa remained consistent and was strengthened to some extent. Johnson's Great Society envisioned domestic programmes to end racial injustice at home and this was very much related to the issue of apartheid in South Africa and to United States policy itself. However, under Johnson, South West Africa (Namibia) rather than South Africa received more attention.[3] The administration continued the policies of the previous administration of neither encouraging nor discouraging American investment and also strengthened the observance of the voluntary arms embargo by refusing the sale of "gray area" material that could be used for both military and civilian purposes (*South Africa: Time Running Out*, 1981, p.350). Afro-Asian efforts at imposing economic sanctions against South Africa received a cool response, prompting the General Assembly's Special Committee on Apartheid placing much of the blame for the failure of its efforts on countries like the United States. Efforts of the Committee to include the United States as a member also proved to be a failure. The United States opposed the majority's decision in the United Nations to label apartheid "aggression" under Chapter VII of the Charter. In the nuclear field US-South African co-operation continued and was specifically manifested by granting to South Africa in 1965 a nuclear reactor and by renewing the nuclear energy agreement in 1967. Contacts of a military and intelligence nature continued as before.

One incident that brought petty apartheid to the realm of foreign affairs was when the American aircraft carrier USS *Franklin Delano Roosevelt* was scheduled to stop at Cape Town on its way from Vietnam, to refuel and give its crew shore leave. Much publicity was given in the American media on the segregated facilities to be offered to the crew. The issue created such an uproar in the United States, that the captain of the carrier had to refuse his crew permission to go ashore and only the refuelling facility was made use of. As a consequence, American naval ships called on South African ports only in emergencies (*South Africa: Time Running Out,* 1981, p.350). The United States also restrained from encouraging exchange programmes between the two countries because of the South African insistence on segregated audiences.

During the latter half of his presidency, Johnson spoke more against apartheid. To mark the third anniversary of the founding of the Organisation of African Unity, he invited a group of African ambassadors to the White House, on which occasion he made the first major presidential address in American history devoted exclusively to African issues. Johnson made clear his aversion to the narrow minded and outmoded policy in some parts of Africa which permitted minority dominance over the majority.

Officials of the administration at the same time admitted that the United States had no prescription for South Africa. What it could do was only persuade while keeping open the lines of contact. On the question of the cessation of investment they thought that it would harden South African policies even further, forcing South Africa to turn to other sources of investment as well as to accelerate its already considerable efforts to achieve economic self sufficiency.

The United States was following a policy that was described as "passive acceptance" or "reluctant concern" (Nielsen, 1969, p.311; *The Dynamics of World Power*, 1973, p.1031). Time and again general policy statements were contradicted by actions and it looked like nothing but hypocrisy to the rest of the world. Critics of American policy wanted the United States to begin the process of disengagement with South Africa because both morally and strategically it represented a sound policy. By 1968, indecision turned out to be the hallmark of American policy towards South Africa. The arms embargo was proving to be ineffective and American equipment continued to be exported to South Africa with or without the knowledge of the Department of Commerce. The administration, however, continued to reiterate that it was scrupulously adhering to the terms of the embargo and complained that South Africa was receiving the latest sophisticated weapons from other sources, which never caught the attention of the critics of the United States (Goldberg, 1968, p.94).

The Johnson administration did not make much progress on South Africa because it could not decide how to influence the process. Moreover, it was trapped by the ambiguities of its own policy. It did not want to encounter a situation in which Blacks challenged White supremacy, and made its own non-interventionist posture even more contentious. American policy lost its credibility because it could not deliver what it promised. Words were not accompanied by deeds. The New Frontier and Great Society failed to bring change in United States policy. The half-hearted American attempt of siding with Third World nations in criticising South Africa remained at rhetoric, far from reality.

In retrospect it can be observed that the United States began showing greater interest in South Africa commensurate with its role as a super power only in 1945. Until then isolationism kept American interests at the non-political level. The foreign policy objectives in the post-war period were related to the overall American interest in containing Communism and denying the Soviet Union a stronghold in areas like Southern Africa. To a great extent the policies of its European allies guided United States policy. Kennedy's and Johnson's policies were only slightly different from Eisenhower's middle of the road policy. The only significant success in American policy towards South Africa in the nineteen sixties was the voluntary arms embargo of 1963. Vietnam had become a major American preoccupation, obscuring all other foreign policy issues. Southern Africa, at the end of the sixties, still remained low on the list of American priorities.

Notes

1. The Union of South Africa came into existence only in 1910 with the merger of Cape, Natal, Transvaal and Orange Free State. The expression "South Africa" in this context would mean any or all of these territories.
2. However, not many committed liberals were appointed to high posts because Kennedy considered them too ideological, zealous and talkative.
3. In 1966 the United States took the leading role in drafting a General Assembly resolution which declared that South Africa had no right to administer Namibia and that henceforth the territory came under the direct responsibility of the United Nations.

4 The Nixon Administration and the Policy of Communication

When Richard Nixon entered the White House in 1969, South Africa was not a high priority foreign policy area for the United States. The previous year had witnessed the Tet offensive in Vietnam and the march of Warsaw Pact troops into Czechoslovakia. While the former converted many Americans to the belief that war could not always be brought to a desired conclusion, the latter convinced them of the American inability to influence events in Eastern Europe. Since the focus of American foreign policy was on places like Southeast Asia and Europe, Southern Africa did not figure prominently in the American agenda.

The new administration assumed office at a time when changes were taking place both internally in the United States as well as globally. Nixon, well known for his anti-Communist posture, had however realised that the international environment had changed and that policies that would serve American interests in peace had to be adopted. Moreover Nixon wanted to fulfil his ambition to create the image of a diplomatist. He did not want history to remember him as a warmonger but a man of peace. Henry Kissinger, Nixon's Special Assistant for National Security Affairs and later Secretary of State writes in his memoirs that Nixon wanted to be remembered as a peacemaker (Kissinger, 1981a, p.414). Kissinger's role itself in the shaping of American foreign policy in the first half of the nineteen seventies was second to none. He states that he came into office at a time when an overhaul of American foreign policy was called for. One of the major problems of the administration was how to orient American policies in such a way as to avoid oscillations on the one hand between excessive moralism and excessive pragmatism and on the other between excessive concern with power and total rejection of power (Graebner, 1984, p.250).

What the administration wanted was the creation of a more constructive future based on the maintenance of the balance of power. The consequence of this thinking ultimately led to détente or the relaxation of tension with the Soviet Union. In short, what was envisaged was an order in which neither the United States nor the Soviet Union would attempt to assert its primacy. It would also be one in which responsibilities would be shared by the nations of the world so as to regulate violence and economic disruption. From the American point of view the importance of détente flowed from two factors. First of all there was a growing popular desire within the United States to limit its involvement in world affairs, as the country was becoming increasingly vulnerable economically. Secondly, it was widely acknowledged that the Soviet Union had acquired strategic parity with the United States and the former's influence particularly in the Third World was on the increase. However, for the United States détente was not exactly a rejection of the Cold War. It was rather a technique or tactic designed to continue the Cold War by other means until the time arrived when it could assert once more its power internationally.

The Nixon Doctrine was a product of the new thinking which asserted that the United States was disinclined to be dragged into future Vietnams. The salient features of the doctrine were that henceforth the United States would maintain its global role and some of its accumulated commitments, but in a different manner. In cases of aggression, wherever the United States thought necessary, it would provide military supplies and economic assistance. The threatened nation was however expected to assume the primary responsibility of providing manpower for its defence (Nixon, 1970).

However, whatever was proclaimed about the new policy, Nixon was not prepared to base American policy decisions entirely on the assumption that the Soviet Union had ceased to be a revolutionary power. "Nixonian ground rules were designed to assure not only the safety of the American interests in a still competitive world, but also the continued primacy of the United States" (Graebner, 1978, p.263).

A Low Priority Area

It is in this global context of American foreign policy that the specific policy of the United States towards South Africa in the seventies has to be examined. For the United States, the dominant issue despite détente was its conflict with the Soviet Union. It was a conflict which extended to all parts of the world. Being a global conflict, the success and failure of American performance even in faraway regions could affect the world-wide equilibrium. In the ultimate analysis therefore, even conflict in a "remote area" like Southern Africa was of importance to the United States.

Neither Africa nor South Africa was a priority of the Nixon administration in January 1969. Rothchild (1973, pp.215-240) described American policy towards Africa until the nineteen seventies as being one of "benign neglect". He also states that several constraints had led the United States to adopt a low keyed approach towards Africa and "as a consequence, the emphasis upon stability and gradual change" could "be seen as a consistent theme in American policy from Eisenhower to the present".

Kissinger was familiar with the issues of South Africa. He had seen for himself the nature of the apartheid regime during his visit to that country in the mid sixties. Although he was convinced that the situation was reprehensive, he nevertheless believed that there was nothing much the United States could do about it. Kissinger was not a person to wage a moral crusade let alone recommend one. His major concerns were fascism, which he had experienced in his younger days; and Communism rather than racism. Moreover, his philosophy was that peace could be achieved neither by moral convictions nor practical wisdom alone, but by a combination of the two (Kissinger, 1981b, pp.79-80).

South Africa was however, not totally disregarded by American policymakers. If the country had some importance at all, it was not only based on the fact that it was resource rich or had volatile problems with regional repercussions, but because it had the potential of becoming an arena where the United States would have to confront the Soviet Union. Any American policy therefore had to take into account this factor.

The Air Transport Agreement Issue

Events do not wait for policy decisions. Before it had time to chalk out a policy on South Africa, the Nixon administration encountered an issue involving that country and one handed over by the previous administration. It was related to the Air Transport Agreement between the two countries, the background of which has to be explained. In 1947, before the National Party had come to power in South Africa and before apartheid had become the national policy, the United States had granted South African Airways (SAA) landing rights in New York with the exact routes to be determined later. Almost two decades later, towards the end of the Johnson administration, South Africa came forward to claim its side of the bargain. It requested that the air routes to New York be specifically mentioned in the Agreement. The United States was confronted with the choice of either honouring the commitment or putting at risk continued air service between the two countries. The administration after introspection arrived at the conclusion that the United States would gain nothing by reneging. On the other hand, in the absence of direct air service, the traffic between the two countries would be shifted to the carriers of other countries that served South Africa. By honouring commitments, the administration concluded, the economic interests of the United States could be safeguarded (*South Africa and United States Foreign* Policy, 1969, pp.17-21). It was assumed that a decision otherwise was not going to make any impact on the course of apartheid. Eventually the Nixon administration inherited the issue from its predecessor.

In January 1969, as soon as the new administration assumed office, both President Nixon and the Civil Aeronautics Board received letters from the American Committee on Apartheid (ACA) requesting that the South African case be reopened. The President's assistant, Robert Ellsworth replied that it was not within the President's power to reopen the case at that moment. This was because of the fact that in keeping with the general rule, permits or certificates of convenience and necessity could not be recalled after the time for reconsideration of the action had expired, and more importantly because the authorisation had come into effect. The SAA had by then started operating on the new route and the period of reconsideration had expired on November 29, 1968. The Civil Aeronautics Board also replied to the ACA that it did not deem it appropriate to take further action (*South Africa and United States Foreign Policy,* 1969, pp.2-3). The Nixon administration was not inclined to get too involved in the controversy. An official of the administration justified its position on the grounds that it was important to keep open the lines of communication for the purpose of closer contact leading to constructive influence. It was necessary to keep in touch with many people in South Africa; White and non-White, who questioned the direction of the policy of apartheid. The administration made it clear that it did not believe that racial repression would disappear if a policy of economic quarantine and isolation was followed (*South Africa and United States Foreign Policy*, 1969, pp.17-21).

Thus, even before it could examine in detail the nature of existing policy or formulate a concrete policy on South Africa, the administration expressed the view that it could not sever its links, particularly because there were economic dimensions to the question. Critics of the administration like Congressman Ogden B. Reid asserted that there was no justification for the administration's position. The permit was granted in 1947, before apartheid had become the national policy of the South African government and no route had been defined on that occasion. There was no justification for granting any route especially the most direct one between New York and Johannesburg to an airline operated by a government intent on perpetuating injustice. Reid also expressed concern that the airline would extend its discriminatory policies towards American citizens. This was a well placed concern given the fact that about 13 per cent of the citizens of the United States were non-White (*South Africa and United States Foreign Policy*, 1969, p.73).

Simultaneously, statements emanating from the administration indicated that the United States was committed to certain American goals. In a statement to the Senate Committee on Foreign Relations, Secretary of State William P. Rogers (1969, p.311) stated:

> Progress in the Southern part of Africa also remains a vital goal of the new African states and one with which we basically sympathise. Self-determination, majority rule with minority rights, and human equality are the products of our own practical experience and our practical idealism; it will be our policy to support them in Africa as well. Our dedication to these goals is the result of our history, a product of our search for basic answers to human aspirations.

Actions of the administration did not fully reflect these sentiments and the administration had its own justification for this. For instance, at the United Nations in July 1969 the United States opposed a Security Council resolution on Southern Rhodesia which called for an extension of economic sanctions to South Africa and Portugal.[1] The American argument was that such a move would not be productive in dealing with the situation. Charles Yost, the American representative stated that sanctions on neighbouring countries just because they were not adequately or successfully applied to Rhodesia seemed to the United States a dubious course introducing additional complications to an already complicated situation (Yost, 1969, p.58). The administration was reluctant either to involve itself in the affairs of Southern Africa or to take a position in favour of the resolution. Both the Air Transport Agreement issue and that of the extension of sanctions were portents of the Nixon administration's South Africa policy which was to be given a concrete shape later.

National Security Study Memorandum 39

An interdepartmental review of American policy towards Southern Africa was initiated by Kissinger in April 1969. Accordingly a National Security Council Group for Africa consisting of the representatives of the Department of State, the Department of Defense, the Central Intelligence Agency and assisted by other departments and agencies was constituted. A careful reading of the situation however reveals that this was not any indication that Southern Africa had suddenly attained importance in United States foreign policy. On the contrary, the review called for was only one among the one hundred and thirty eight such reviews on different regions and issues of the world that would be assigned by Kissinger during the period between January 1969 and October 1971.[2] For Kissinger, the study of Southern Africa was necessitated by his conviction that it was an area where American policy was meandering aimlessly and unproductively under the influence of a client oriented Department of State. He felt that American interests were not being taken care of by those at Foggy Bottom. Kissinger wanted policy concerning the area to be put in order and made realistic enough so that decision makers in the administration could concentrate on other things without being disturbed by the distractions of Southern Africa (*South Africa: Time Running Out*, 1981, p.350).

Much information regarding the inner working of the Group comes from Roger Morris, Senior Staff Assistant to Kissinger in the National Security Council (Morris, 1977, pp.107-120). Morris writes that the response to Southern Africa in the administration had been to avoid to a great extent any thinking about the harsh questions it posed. The Nixon administration had inherited a policy that amounted to the "shifting sum of contradictory bureaucratic interests pursued on an adhoc basis". On the one hand the Department of State took a pro-Black African stand in the United Nations by lauding the imposition of sanctions on Rhodesia and by verbal ostracism of the White regimes. On the other hand the Central Intelligence Agency maintained close professional ties with the anti-Communist security services of the White regimes, the Department of Commerce encouraged profitable trade with them, the National Aeronautics and Space Administration (NASA) ran a segregated space station in South Africa and the United States Navy made use of the refuelling facilities at Cape Town. There was no American policy, only policies, reflective of the hypocrisy in the country's foreign policy. This was what Kissinger wanted to rectify.

But to organise policy towards the region was not an easy task. As Morris states, two factors limited realistic options. First of all, no President, particularly a conservative like Nixon could be expected in 1969 to abandon the significant material interests in the region. Secondly, if the purpose of policy was peaceful change to majority rule, the experience in Southern Africa starting from British colonialism to Rhodesian sanctions had made it clear that external coercion only reinforced the "laager" mentality and unity of the White minorities. An acceptable policy had to take into account these premises. Moreover, such a policy would not only have to recognise the expedient American interests in the oppressive regimes but would also have to make use of the American "presence" wherever possible to influence such regimes to reform their racial systems (Morris, 1977, p.110).

When the National Security Council review was assigned in April 1969, it was scheduled for completion in two weeks. However, it was not forwarded to the Review Group until late November 1969. The text of the National Security Study Memorandum 39 (NSSM 39) as it was known, opened with a brief review of American interests and policy in Southern Africa. It emphasised specific measures initiated both inside and outside the United States by previous administrations in response to the outbreak of the national liberation struggle in Southern Africa. A comparison was made between American policy on the one hand and British and French policies on the other in an attempt to extol the former. Mention was made of the global realities the United States had to face while formulating policy, including the strategic importance of Southern Africa, military facilities for the United States in the context of the Indo-China war, significant American investment and balance of trade advantages, and South Africa's status as the major world supplier of gold (El Khawas and Cohen, 1976).

The predicament of the United States over its conflicting interests as well as the possibility of jeopardising American relations with the rest of Africa over Southern Africa was illuminated in the study. The objectives of United States policy towards Southern Africa were outlined in it. These objectives included improvement of the American policy on racial issues, minimising violence in Southern Africa, reducing opportunities for Communist powers to meddle in the region for their own benefit, encouraging the moderation of existing policies of White regimes and protecting American economic and strategic interests in the region. The National Security Council staff while reviewing existing policy arrived at the conclusion that "communication" was preferable to "confrontation".

The most important section of the document was the one which outlined policy alternatives for the Nixon administration. Five policy options were specified. A background to each option was followed by a broad policy position and supported by operational examples. The section concluded with the pros and cons associated with each option. At the final meeting of the National Security Council in December 1969 the five policy options were submitted for discussion. Option One called for closer relations with the White regimes so that American economic and strategic interests could be better protected. Option Two suggested closer association with South Africa with the intention of persuading it to reform the apartheid system. Option Three envisaged strictly limited co-operation with South Africa with the intention of safeguarding American interests while adopting simultaneously a position acceptable to international opinion. While Option Four called for dissociation from South Africa and closer relations with Black nationalists, Option Five entailed dissociation from both sides so that American involvement could be limited.

Each option had advantages as well as disadvantages. Out of the five options, Option Three was the one followed by the two previous administrations. Its acceptance meant continuation of the old policy. Moreover, Option Three was considered to be a blend of moral overtones and diplomatic appeal. Since it did not preclude giving up American interests, there was the possibility of Option Three being widely criticised as expedient and hypocritical.

Option One was based on the assumption that the United States could have no influence on the developments in the region. It was an option which took for granted the status quo in the region. The views of Dean Acheson, former Secretary of State, had influenced the drafting of this option. Acheson regarded condemnation of racist regimes as a sign of extreme moralism in diplomacy (Morris, 1977, p.113). But how far did moral concerns influence policy in the Nixon administration? It has been stated that neither the Department of State nor the National Security Council believed that the United States could remain morally uncommitted. Contrary to popular perception the Nixon administration took the ethical argument very seriously (Coker, 1986, p.23). Kissinger briefed Nixon with a special paper entitled "Domestic and Moral Factors in Southern Africa". The thrust of the paper, argued philosophically, was that "racial tyranny was the most odious for being inescapable at birth". It also warned that American policy towards the White regimes could turn out to be a volatile issue in American politics (Morris, 1977, p.114). Option One was not considered realistic enough because it did not take into account the existing intricacies of global power equations. The Soviet Union and China had made inroads into Southern Africa and were supporting liberation movements fighting White regimes. Above all the option would not receive public approval in the United States where it would be opposed particularly by Afro-Americans and liberals.

Options Four and Five had one thing in common with Option One. They called for either total disengagement or total support of one party in the conflict. Their utility was seen to be in an academic or intellectual context rather than in actual practice. Option Four was diametrically opposed to Option One. There was no reason to believe that the supporters of the Nixon administration including industrialists, multinational corporations or conservatives would approve of its total association with the Black liberation movements. Moreover, it meant driving a wedge between the United States and its profitable trade and investment in South Africa and access to the minerals and strategic facilities of the region. Option Five called for a new brand of American isolationism vis à vis Southern Africa. It was meant to limit American involvement by dissociating from both the White regimes as well as Black nationalists.

The first, fourth and fifth options were dispensed with early in the deliberations. Option Three also met with the same fate as it had been followed by the previous administrations and also because it was the Department of States' pet option. Given the Nixon administration's disapproval of punitive measures as well as existing sanctions, coupled with its belief that sanctions were ineffective; the Option had no chance of being adopted.

It was clear that the focus would rest on Option Two. In the memorandum itself, the National Security Council staff had devoted more time and energy to the discussion of this option which made it clear that it was their obvious choice. Option Two proceeded on the following premise:

> The whites are here to stay and the only way that constructive change can come about is through them. There is no hope for the blacks to gain the political rights they seek through violence. . . . We can, through selective relaxation of our stance toward the white regimes, encourage some modification of their current racial and colonial policies. . . . Our tangible interests form a basis for our contacts in the region, and these can be maintained at an acceptable political cost. (El Khawas and Cohen, 1976, p.105)

The Tar Baby Option, as the document came to be known, was subsequently leaked and published in full. The document assumed that American interests in Southern Africa were "important" rather than "vital", while at the same time it portrayed an image of not being supportive of apartheid. The acceptance of Option Two over other options was based on certain realities of the region. In Southern Rhodesia, the nationalist movement was divided and guerrilla activity had slackened. Moreover the Rhodesian economy was flourishing. South Africa also was prospering economically and converting itself into an invulnerable military fortress. The Portuguese were still in control of their colonies in Angola and Mozambique. There were no signs to indicate the end of White rule in Southern Africa. These factors strengthened the case for Option Two which was eventually approved by President Nixon.

Nixon received the standard decision memorandum from Kissinger towards the end of 1969. It recommended that the United States maintain a low profile in the United Nations when issues involving apartheid and minority rule were being discussed and also to adopt a less doctrinaire approach to bilateral problems with South Africa. It also recommended to reduce pressure on the Portuguese and to grant increased aid to the Black states of Southern Africa. It was also decided to relax the arms embargo of 1963 and extend trade promotion to American firms exporting to South Africa.

The outcome of the NSSM 39 exercise was the subordination of concerns like apartheid and human rights to tangible interests of an economic and strategic nature. At the bureaucratic level within the United States, the scales tilted in favour of the Departments of Defense and Commerce as well as business constituencies; to the detriment of the Department of State and liberal constituencies (*South Africa: Time Running Out*, 1981, p.352). It has been pointed out that Nixon and Kissinger were largely responsible for the demise of the Department of State as a vital policymaking unit in the foreign policy process. They strengthened other units at the expense of the Department of State.

The United States wanted South Africa to remain the dominant power in Southern Africa, one which would maintain close relations with its Black neighbours and act as a regional surrogate. A conducive environment was essential for the relaxation of tension, the absence of violence and consequently, the protection of American interests. Simultaneously the United States sought to improve its relations with Black Africa. In short, the United States seemed to be prepared for any political arrangement except majority rule. There was of course the possibility of the Soviet Union and China exploiting the situation. But this concern was to be subordinated for the time being to American economic and strategic interests. These interests were considered the basis of American policy towards the region and they could be "maintained at an acceptable political cost". The thinking that the American approach would induce modification in the policy of apartheid was in contrast to the Tar Baby Option's assertion that the existing thrust of South Africa's domestic policy did not envisage any basic change in the system of apartheid. The document itself admitted that there was no evidence that change would occur in South African policies as a result of American policy. Goldsworthy (1980, p.224) states:

> But beneath this apparent doublethink what mattered was that Option Two dictated a strategy (never officially stated as such) of recognising, dealing with, and discreetly supporting the established power-holders in Southern Africa. Tar-Baby was principally designed, of course, to serve American interests rather than to preserve white rule as such, but in the circumstances the latter was seen as a necessary corollary of the former.

Option Two in short was unrealistic and one that displayed indifference to the legitimate aspirations of the African people. The "cynical lack of concern" stood out "in marked contrast to the public platitudes and rhetoric of American spokesmen" (Martin and Johnson, 1981, p.230).

The Policy of Communication

NSSM 39 remained a secret document until it was eventually leaked. At the same time American policy towards Southern Africa was shaped and guided on its basis. Without acknowledging the existence of such a document, the administration declared it had formulated a policy that was based on the view that closer ties with South Africa would encourage moderation of apartheid and that increased pressure on it would not in any case change the course of apartheid. This was the new American policy of communication, the main advocate of which was David Newsom, Assistant Secretary of State for African Affairs. He stated:

> We believe that appropriate channels of communication and dialogue must be kept open. We believe contact with the outside world will help the non-

> white majorities and will help bring the white rulers to an understanding of the need for a change in their policies. (Newsom, 1970, p.423)

The policy of communication turned out to be beneficial to those within the administration like the Pentagon, Department of Commerce, Central Intelligence Agency, and the National Aeronautics and Space Administration as well as private business interests. They could continue their strategic and economic ties with South Africa while racial confrontation still continued there. Sir Seretse Khama, President of Botswana, while addressing the African-American Dialogue, in Lagos, made a critical assessment of American policy. He pointed out that peaceful change would not be secured if existing minority ruled situations were allowed to harden and South Africa's outward movement encouraged. While suggesting separate solutions for the problems of Southern Africa, Khama said:

> This involves restraining South Africa's outward expansion, eroding the outward edges of the white bastion developing in Southern Africa, driving wedges between its constituent parts, preventing its further consolidation, and maintaining contact and communication with all the forces for change throughout the region. Unless a positive overall strategy is developed along these lines, then communication will slip into acceptance and moral pressure will be reduced to mere rhetoric. (*The Dynamics of World Power*, 1973, pp.951-956)

The administration, early in 1970, decided to increase communication and selective involvement with the White regimes of Southern Africa. Since their stability was recognised, the administration tilted in their favour. The change became apparent not through any policy statement but through operational examples.

It had been the policy of the United States until then to enforce the arms embargo of 1963. However, services like repair and engine replacement for aircraft sold before 1963 were not affected by the embargo since they did not come under its purview. South Africa was able to overcome the effects of the embargo for instance by using for military purposes, aircraft that were sold to commercial consignees. The administration diluted existing restrictions by relaxing the sale of "gray area" equipment which could be used for both civilian and military purposes. American multinationals were permitted to sell defence related equipment. IBM sold four computers to the South African Department of Defence. The Foxboro Company of Massachusetts was permitted in 1973 to sell two large computers which were then used to run a secret uranium enrichment plant near Pretoria (Talbott, 1977, p.13). American military aircraft made routine use of both South African airforce bases and civilian airports.

Changes were visible in the financial sphere too. In 1970 the United States Export Import Bank (EXIMBANK) extended the term of insurance available to finance exports to South Africa from five to ten years.[3] There was a four fold expansion in medium term insurance issued in 1970 and 1971 compared to the previous four years. Trade and investment statistics show that they had been facilitated and encouraged (Lockwood, 1974, p.66).

It became the policy of the Nixon administration to conduct selected exchange programmes with South Africa in all spheres including defence. The visits to the United States included not only those by influential moderate South African Black and Coloured leaders but also by top ranking political and military figures of the South African government. The policy of previous administrations to limit military contacts was discontinued and private visits by South African officials on military business were permitted. In January 1974, Cornelius Mulder, the South African Minister for Information met Deputy Assistant Secretary of Defense, Admiral Ray Peet as well as Vice President Ford. In May 1974, the chief of the South African Defence Force (SADF) Admiral Hugo Biermann met Admiral Thomas Moorer, Chairman of the Joint Chiefs of Staff and J. W. Middendorf, Acting Secretary of the Navy.

On the political and diplomatic front, in the United Nations, condemnation of apartheid and the illegal South African control of Namibia was replaced by abstentions, while abstentions on resolutions requiring action were replaced by opposition. A conservative businessman from Texas, John G. Hurd was appointed the ambassador to South Africa. In the words of a Department of State official, he "could be expected to establish a rapport with the South African establishment that his predecessors deliberately avoided" (Johnson, 1973, p.22). South Africa also benefited during this period from certain American decisions taken on a different issue namely the pricing of gold. To finance the deficit arising out of the Vietnam war, the administration decided to let the price of gold float above $35 an ounce. This turned out to be a boon for South Africa because the price went up to about $200 an ounce. Moreover, South Africa was also permitted to sell gold to the International Monetary Fund (IMF). The decision insulated South Africa substantially against international recession and economic crisis and enabled it to earn about $307 million from gold sales to the IMF in the first half of 1970 (Johnson, 1973, p.22).

Despite these decisions, South Africa did not obtain unlimited attention from American policy planners. The preoccupation with Vietnam and the American withdrawal from there made it unlikely that political capital would be spent on publicly reversing the policy on South Africa. American strategists did not formulate an active concept of a South African strategy and the basic strategic concerns of both countries remained different. Nixon and Kissinger indirectly suggested to South Africa that there was a change in policy advantageous to the latter. But the American stance in the United Nations of being critical of apartheid was disapproved by the South Africans. Kissinger expected the South Africans to appreciate his deeds rather than believe his words. Even his allusions that the position taken by the American ambassador to the United Nations was not a reflection of the administration's actual policy, failed to convince the South Africans. For them harsh words undermined whatever influence was gained by the arms sales (Bissel, 1982, p.56). The South Africans came to realise that the American bark was worse than the American bite.

The Nixon administration, without revealing actual policy criticised apartheid through its public statements. At the same time it advocated closer contact to influence South Africa. It also publicly discounted the threat of Communism to developing countries particularly in Africa. The reason it cited was that the Communist world lacked unity and had failed to prove itself in the sphere of economic development. However, in NSSM 39 the Communist threat had been highlighted.

At a time when the administration was busy drafting NSSM 39, the Fifth Summit Conference of East and Central African States was held in Lusaka. The summit attended by thirteen states issued a declaration on Southern Africa better known as the Lusaka Manifesto. In a conciliatory tone it offered South Africa a reasonable timetable for majority rule provided it publicly committed itself to introducing it. It was not a severe but rather a passionately reasoned condemnation of apartheid. An important characteristic of the manifesto was its tone, which called for peaceful instead of violent change in Southern Africa. Although it was eulogised throughout the world, the Nixon administration did not comment on it when it was issued. Congressmen like Senator Edward Kennedy called on the administration to make it clear to the signatories that the United States supported their position and that it opposed racial discrimination in Southern Africa just as Americans opposed it in the United States (Kennedy, 1969, pp.6083-6084). Other critics of the administration included Representatives Charles Diggs and Lester L. Wolff. In a report following a special study mission to Southern Africa, they described American policy as "schizophrenic". They criticised the policy for its double standards. On the one hand, they said, the United States was committed to freedom and equality and opposed to tyranny and justice, while on the other hand it made an "immoral entangling alliance" with South Africa through its economic, space, aviation and other links. The report further stated that:

> US self-interest is dramatized by the presence in our midst of over 25 million black citizens who are increasingly identifying with their cultural heritage and who are on the threshold of linking up with the goals of the African liberation movement. . . . If it is to be on the side of the vast majority of Africans, our present policies and plans should reflect an enlightened projection and drastic revisions are demanded. (*Report of Special Study Mission to Southern Africa,* 1969, pp.2-6)

The reluctance of the administration to pursue a strict approach was evident during the controversy surrounding the Afro-American tennis player Arthur Ashe. Ashe was denied a visa by the South African government when he applied for it to participate in the South African National Tennis Championships. It was evident that he was denied the visa because he happened to be an Afro-American. The administration refused to reciprocate by retaliatory visa refusal to South African athletes who wanted to visit the United States. It considered such a policy correct in relation to American values, one which portrayed the United States positively in comparison with South Africa. The administration however stated that it was in South Africa's deepest interest to foster foreign contacts and exchange, not to shut itself off in sterile isolation (*Foreign Policy Implications of Racial Exclusion in Granting Visas*, 1970, pp.1-4).

Senior officials in the administration reiterated the importance of American ideals and values. William P. Rogers, Secretary of State, on his visit to Africa stated that the United States opposed systems based on racial discrimination in Africa because of America's own heritage and moral principles. He pointed out that while there was full agreement on the principle, there were different points of view on how to achieve the results (Rogers, 1970a, p.376). Following his visit, Rogers submitted a statement to President Nixon in which he said that the problems of Southern Africa were extremely stubborn, passions were strong and no easy solutions were in sight. The United States did not believe in severing relations with South Africa because it would not advance the course it pursued or help the majority of the people. The limited governmental activities that the United

States pursued in South Africa, he said, did not mean the acceptance of its discriminatory system. At the same time the administration could not accept the fatalistic view that violence could ultimately resolve these issues. Rogers reiterated that solutions rested in the "constructive interplay of political, economic and social forces" which would inevitably lead to change (Rogers, 1970b, pp.520-521). Rogers outlined the administration's new Africa policy. The policy emphasised firstly, support for self-determination rooted in America's own traditions of independence and racial equality. Secondly, it emphasised the desire for more economic relations. Rogers stated that it was in accordance with the first precept that the United States had been maintaining an arms embargo on South Africa and discouraging investments in Namibia as long as South Africa continued to rule the territory.

While occasionally issuing statements on Africa and South Africa in particular, the administration made efforts to downgrade the importance of Southern African issues. Assistant Secretary Newsom said that they were not as primary as those of the Middle East but were related to the problems of long range concern in the developing world. No African problem, he admitted, had demanded and received greater attention from his administration than the problem of Southern Africa. He however, was against mandatory economic sanctions in the case of South Africa on the grounds that they were neither practicable nor likely to advance American goals (Newsom, 1970, p.419).

The Polaroid Initiative

In contrast to the administration's attitudes, some American multinationals took a direct and positive stand on apartheid. These companies did not want to terminate their business in South Africa. At the same time they did not want to conform with the system of apartheid. As a compromise between the two extremes, they took steps to attract greater public attention to the issue of employment practices and conditions in South Africa. The Polaroid Corporation for instance, undertook an experimental programme in relation to its business activities there. It decided to raise the wages of its non-White employees, initiate training programmes for non-White employees to undertake greater responsibilities, and to commit a portion of its profits earned in South Africa to encourage Black education.[4] It also decided to investigate the possibility of creating a Black managed company in one or more of the Black African nations. Polaroid raised the wages of its Black employees by between 17 per cent and 33 per cent. It also decided to withdraw the sale of products which could be used directly or indirectly in enforcing apartheid (*Southern Africa: Proposals for Americans*, 1971, p.47). Until the Polaroid experiment, no multinational corporation had sought to challenge the system of apartheid. They rather conformed to it and profited from it. The Polaroid initiative, though not comprehensive, was widely welcomed by the detractors of apartheid as a first step towards challenging it.

But the experiment did not create the impact it was expected to. It did not have the desired effect on the administration which continued to highlight the importance of foreign investment. The administration left the initiative to corporations to decide for themselves what they should do in South Africa.[5] David Newsom (1972, p.445) commenting on the experiment said that it was a matter essentially between American business and its employees in the countries of Southern Africa. He said that the Department of State, however, stood ready to counsel with American firms on things that could be done consistent with the laws of the foreign land in which they operated. In his report to Congress in February 1971, Nixon (1971, p.388) stated that his administration would do what it could to encourage the White regimes to adopt more generous and realistic policies towards Black citizens. At the same time the administration, just as it could not condone the violence to human dignity implicit in apartheid, could not also associate with those who called for violent solutions. Violence, he stated, would only harden the resistance of the "White revolutionaries" to evolutionary change.

The Sugar Quota Issue

The Sugar Quota issue figured prominently in American policy during 1971. The quota was a form of direct support or subsidy by the United States government to the South African government. In 1971, both the House of Representatives and the Senate approved a bill that permitted South Africa to sell over 57,000 tons of sugar, which was about 6.5 per cent of its crop, for three years in a protected American market at double the world price. Several circles within the United States regarded the move as one which reflected the American tolerance of the practice of indentured labour in the South African sugar sector. An attempt to cancel the quota was narrowly defeated in the Senate. Speaking before the House, Representative John Dow (1971, pp.2414-2415) pointed out that it was the most appropriate time to discuss the policy of continuing support by economic means to a government which practised racial discrimination which was repugnant to the principles and ideals of all Americans. Dow stated that while apartheid was being deplored by American officials, no governmental act had followed these pronouncements.

The administration took no heed of such criticism. Although the President was empowered to revoke the quota, the administration went only to the extent of promising that over the next four years it would review the allocation and arrangements. *The New York Times,* in an editorial stated that this "foreign aid" to a highly advanced country with a booming economy, one which practised a "virulent brand of racial discrimination", was one of the many disgraceful effects of the United States Sugar Act of 1948.[6]

Carrots, not sticks, were used by the administration while dealing with the South African apartheid regime. The administration's real concern was for American investments in South Africa. It reiterated time and again that the ability of the United States to bring about change in South Africa was limited. The object of the policy of communication was peaceful evolutionary change, not retaliation or punishment. American private investment, in the opinion of the administration, had a positive effect. It added to economic pressure to bring more non-Whites into the labour force at increasingly higher levels. It increased contact with the outside world through foreign businessmen and technicians and provided an opportunity to start enlightened employment policies to improve the well-being of and opportunities for non-Whites. It also served as a channel through which outside influence could be felt as was evident in the case of the Polaroid experiment. In essence, all these things could be reduced to two statements. Firstly, the United States government neither encouraged nor discouraged new investment in South Africa. Secondly, existing investment, if properly managed, could contribute to peaceful and constructive change in South Africa (Smith, 1971, pp.825-827).

The Black Caucus and the Administration

Afro-American Congressmen led by Charles Diggs, who had formed the Congressional Black Caucus to advance issues of concern to their community, were strong critics of the administration's policy towards South Africa. Diggs (1971, p.4646) remarked that he did not find the administration's advocacy of the use of communication to support peaceful change persuasive. He found no evidence that the policy of communication was pursued to establish links with the majority Black South Africans and liberal elements who wished to see peaceful change in South Africa. Diggs also happened to be a member of the United States delegation to the United Nations. In December 1971 he resigned from the delegation over the administration's attitude on Southern Africa. As a first hand witness, he found "stifling, the hypocrisy" of the United States government, "which while uttering its abhorrence of apartheid, unflaggingly" voted "in opposition to any attempt to act, rather than orate, with respect to apartheid and minority regimes of Southern Africa". Diggs alleged that the United States mission to the United Nations had lost out to the European bureau of the Department of State, economic and military groups and other "watchdogs" of Southern African policy (*The Dynamics of World Power*, 1973, p.959). In an editorial, *The New York Times* stated that Diggs should neither have taken seriously the administration's rhetoric against apartheid, nor its promises to consult members of the delegation in advance about the positions to be taken in the General Assembly. Commenting on the American policy itself, the editorial pointed out that it was "part of an emerging pattern of far greater Washington concern for the sensibilities of white rulers of Southern Africa" rather than for the Blacks who were struggling for justice and self-determination.[7]

The administration's double standards were reflected in its voting record at the United Nations. On several issues it sided with the minority regimes against the interests of the majority Blacks. It consistently refused to label apartheid a crime against humanity. The Nixon administration failed to recognise the nature and potential of the race problem in South Africa. It spoke of neutrality which amounted to double talk. Throughout South Africa, American officials were encouraging trade and investment, supplying the regime with necessary information and "mixing with all the 'right' people such as the Vorsters, the Schoemans and the Mulders", all of which led to "a steady retrogression".[8]

In 1972, when Nixon was re–elected, it meant a continuation of the existing policy for another four years. One observer predicted that the confrontation between Nixon and Diggs would grow into one of major proportions. He warned that a section of the American population would not remain silent if an insensitive President with casual callousness involved the United States in the "wrong side of another series of wars of national liberation" (Oudes, 1973, pp.32-33). Kissinger's appointment as Secretary of State in 1973 strengthened his position vis à vis foreign policy decision making. At his confirmation hearings before the Senate, he admitted that on the issues of Africa the United States had to allow Europe the leading role since it was occupied with other areas like Southeast Asia. Once these concerns were over, it could shift attention to sub Saharan Africa and from then onwards one would see more energy devoted to these problems (Kissinger, 1974, p.233). Two months later Donald Easum was appointed the Assistant Secretary of State for African Affairs.

Watergate obscured several domestic and foreign policy issues in 1974. Events finally culminated in Nixon's resignation. By then, in the context of South Africa, the administration was still occupied with the issue whether foreign investment could act as a catalyst for economic growth and help reduce the economic disparities between Black and White labour. It had also just begun considering whether the Black labour force would be able to negotiate with the regime directly without the intercession of an external power (Coker, 1986, p.86).

The Nixon administration engaged in rhetoric which justified the need for racial justice, self-determination and majority rule based on American ideals. But it did not want to use its powers in a manner which would affect American economic interests. It did not even extend full support to the efforts of American multinationals when they embarked on their own experiments. The administration was largely unaware of the developments in South Africa, let alone their significance. From the very beginning it believed in pursuing a policy of contact or communication with the White minority regime. Within a year of its assumption of office, it embraced Option Two of NSSM 39 as the lodestar of its Southern Africa policy. Events that took place later in the region show that the analysis was faulty and the assumptions were not based on sound judgement. The administration failed to understand the realities and could not in any significant manner influence South Africa. As a result it bequeathed to the subsequent Ford administration an unrealistic policy, the brunt of which had to be borne by the latter.

Notes

1. The United Nations had imposed mandatory economic sanctions on Rhodesia following the Unilateral Declaration of Independence by the White regime. South Africa and Portugal openly defied them and offered Rhodesia alternative rail and

road access to their ports. Some western countries also benefited from the clandestine trade with Rhodesia.

2. In the first hundred days of the Nixon administration, Kissinger assigned 55 study memoranda or terms papers as they were sometimes called. In 1969, 85 were assigned, 26 in 1970 and 27 during the first nine months of 1971. The one on Southern Africa was ordered on April 10, 1969. See, John P. Leacacos (1971-1972) "Kissinger's Apparat", *Foreign Policy* (Washington, DC), no. 5, pp. 3-27.
3. EXIMBANK is the government agency set up to assist foreign exports. It provides loans to foreign borrowers who wish to buy American goods and services.
4. "An Experiment in South Africa", Advertisement placed by Polaroid in *The New York Times*, January 13, 1971.
5. The Polaroid experiment was also meant to serve as an example to other American companies. But the administration did not throw its full support behind it. Neither did the experiment influence South African labour legislation. In November 1977, it was abandoned and Polaroid terminated its South African business.
6. *The New York Times*, June 8, 1971.
7. *The New York Times*, December 18, 1971.
8. Discussion on paper by Bruce Oudes (1973) "Observations on America's Policy Problems in Southern Africa", *Issue: A Quarterly Journal of Africanist Opinion* (Waltham), vol.3(4), pp. 33-42.

5 Promoting Controlled Change: Priority of the Ford Administration

The Ford administration inherited a Southern Africa policy from the Nixon administration at a point when events having far reaching consequences for American foreign policy were taking place in the region. In the new administration, Henry Kissinger retained his previous position as the Secretary of State. The subsequent history of the Ford administration indicates that he remained the dominant influence in the foreign policy establishment. In Kissinger's words, "one of the more cruel torments of Nixon's Watergate purgatory was my emergence as the pre-eminent figure in foreign policy" (Kissinger, 1981a, p.414). Ford depended more on Kissinger than Nixon had in matters relating to foreign policy. Lukacs (1984, p.79) observes that Kissinger's "rise to this kind of eminence, including his Secretaryship of State, was in itself symptomatic of the transformation of American society and of the decline of those traditional reservoirs wherefrom public servants of the highest ranks had been customarily tapped". Continuity rather than change was the main feature of the Ford administration's foreign policy. This was true particularly as Kissinger continued to exercise his previous role. To a joint session of Congress, Ford pledged continuity in the American dedication to the humane goals which had been a major contribution of the country to mankind (Ford, 1974, p.334).

Even during the Nixon administration, Kissinger had displayed an apparent disposition to view events in the Third World from a strictly bipolar perspective. He felt that the Soviet Union was behind every event which was anti-American in nature. During his second stint as Secretary of State, Kissinger was perhaps even more obsessed with the Cold War, so much so that American interests in a particular region were identified almost completely in terms of Soviet involvement.

United States policy towards Southern Africa was based on Option Two of the National Security Study Memorandum 39 which took for granted the permanence of White regimes in Southern Africa. But the premises on which this was based had already collapsed in 1974 with the developments arising from the Portuguese coup of that year. The Portuguese army's frustration over its Africa policy and the administration of colonies led to the new government's declaration to decolonise. This was a catalyst for the events in Southern Africa which culminated in the independence of Mozambique and the civil war in Angola. The preoccupation of policymakers in Washington with the effort to save Nixon's presidency in the wake of Watergate deprived them of the time and energy to concentrate on the affairs of Southern Africa. Moreover, the situation that arose in Africa after the Portuguese decision was apparently peripheral to the United States' more important concerns like détente and West Asia. By the time Ford and Kissinger settled down to concentrate on Southern Africa, it occurred to them that the premises on which American policy was based had shattered. The Whites in Southern Africa were no longer "here to stay". American policymakers panicked, for the United States could not afford to lose out in the new situation.

Angola: Collusion with South Africa

In Angola the United States decided to back the two pro-west groups namely the National Front for the Liberation of Angola (FNLA) and the National Union for the Total Independence of Angola (UNITA) against the left oriented and Soviet supported Popular Movement for the Liberation of Angola (MPLA). Under Kissinger's guidance the United States plunged into the uncertain and unfathomable abyss of Angola. Instead of accepting the Angolan civil strife as a war of independence, Kissinger defined it as an exploitative Soviet adventure. The lessons of Vietnam had not been properly assimilated. The United States stepped up support for FNLA and UNITA by providing covert assistance amounting to about $30 million by the end of 1975. This assistance, as Kissinger held, was not on the basis of Angola's importance, but on global considerations. In the meantime, South Africa, with encouragement from the United States, began its own incursion into Angola in October 1975. It joined the pro-west factions against the MPLA. For several years South Africa had collaborated with the Portuguese in military and intelligence sectors, and Angola had served as a base from which the South West Africa Peoples Organisation (SWAPO) camps were targeted. Moreover, it also had interests in protecting the Kunene Dam on the Namibia-Angola border.

Covert American aid could not last for long. When funds dried up, the administration approached Congress for money for its Angolan operations. By this time the American clandestine involvement had begun to surface in the American press. Many Congressmen disapproved of covert activity in Angola, pointing out that the administration had embarked on another Vietnam-like war which they could not win. Moreover, they disapproved of secret assistance in a civil war. Collaborating with South Africa too, they thought, would alienate the rest of Black Africa from the United States. Senator Dick Clark, chairman of the Senate Subcommittee on Africa of the Foreign Relations Committee introduced an amendment to a foreign aid authorisation bill to prevent further covert aid. Senator John V. Tunney brought an amendment to the Defense Appropriations Bill to eliminate $33 million which was believed to be earmarked for the Angolan operations. Both amendments were passed and American aid ceased to flow to the pro-western factions.

The South Africans had already advanced into Angolan territory when these developments took place. Undoubtedly they were furious at the American betrayal and were left with no choice but to withdraw. At the Senate hearings on Angola, Kissinger denied any collaboration with South Africa.[1] But on the South African side, people like P. W. Botha, the then Defence Minister affirmed that they had entered with the knowledge and approval of the United States.[2] Angola was a catastrophe for both the United States and South Africa. The United States in particular, "zigzagged crazily between a logically defensible Executive policy of involvement and a logically defensible Congressional policy of disengagement" (Frank and Weisband, 1979, p.57).

The implications of the Angolan fiasco had a profound impact on Kissinger's thinking. His diplomacy was essentially Metternichian and conceived in balance of power terms. The prevailing balance of power between the super powers was not to be affected by any unregulated change. The Soviet role in Angola and its backing of the victorious MPLA represented a violation of the rules. The Soviet success posed a great threat to the prevailing order and the western interests it secured. It looked as though the domino theory would materialise in Southern Africa.[3] Following the Portuguese colonies, the next dominoes could possibly be Rhodesia and Namibia in that order and eventually South Africa. Kissinger perceived that wars of national liberation could result in the transformation of nationalist organisations into ideologically radical groups because of the support they received from the Soviet Union. This was no longer to remain a nightmare but a reality for the United States given the extent of Soviet activity in the region. Taking all these factors into consideration, Kissinger sought to change the image, if not the substance of American policy.

Kissinger's fundamental objective was to ensure the security of South Africa, where the West had its greatest concentration of interests. To him it was in the best interests of the United States to prevent the radicalisation of national movements and prevent "undesirable change". This could be achieved only by promoting controlled democratisation of Rhodesia and Namibia. Moderate African leadership had to be installed in power in both these countries. Simultaneously armed struggle had to be "short circuited" because of the opportunities for intervention that it provided to the Soviet Union. This Kissingerian assessment was also one shared by many South Africans (Goldsworthy, 1980, pp.227-228). Moreover, a lobby in the Pentagon actively supported by South Africa constantly highlighted the importance of that country for the United States. The threat of a near term prospect where South Africa would not only be the "only White regime" but also the "only friendly regime" in the region to the United States was being highlighted. Kissinger was accordingly planning a new approach for the problems of Southern Africa.

The Expulsion Issue and the Disclosure of NSSM 39

Meanwhile apartheid was being condemned internationally. At the United Nations, in October 1974, the United States opposed the move of the majority to expel South Africa from the world body. In the Security Council the United States joined Britain and France in vetoing the resolution. John Scali, the representative of the United States stated that in the American analysis, expulsion of South Africa would only strengthen the racist elements in that country and harden their attitudes. "History holds no example of a pariah state that reformed itself in exile", he said (Scali, 1974, p.777). Scali also pointed out that the ouster would be a strategic mistake at a time when voices of reconciliation were being heard from South Africa.[4] The United States warned that the unprecedented attempt to expel a member from the world body would set a shattering precedent which could gravely damage the United Nations structure. The *Christian Science Monitor* stated that it appreciated the negative votes cast by the western powers and others because ostracising a nation on account of its internal policies was counterproductive.[5]

By the end of 1974, as the South African expulsion issue came to the fore, the details of NSSM 39 began to appear in the press. The revelations affected Kissinger's credibility. The Department of State, also in low profile because of the leak, refused to discuss the implications of NSSM 39. Officials at Foggy Bottom told reporters that it was "nonsense" to suggest that the United States had at any time during the Nixon administration decided to tilt in favour of the White regimes. At the same time, privately, officials were admitting that the disclosure had caused considerable damage. What they could now do was to limit the harm by trying to convince the public that despite the recommendations of NSSM 39, American policy towards Southern Africa had not changed much.

Within the Department of State there were considerable differences between officials and their styles. Many of Kissinger's subordinates did not think in terms of "realpolitik". One such person was Donald Easum, Assistant Secretary of State for African Affairs, who was sworn in just before the Portuguese coup. To create a better image of American foreign policy particularly in the wake of the South African expulsion issue in the General Assembly, Easum undertook an African tour. There was a need to explain the American veto to the Africans and also to put some credibility into the communication policy towards South Africa. But Easum's style was not what Kissinger approved of. Kissinger took exception to Easum's positions and statements and thought that he was too pro-African, myopic and a dull witted bureaucrat (Oudes, 1975, pp.17-19). Kissinger also regarded Easum overzealous when it came to questions of South Africa and apartheid. As early as 1973, responding to complaints from the South African Foreign Minister Hilgard Muller, Kissinger promised to stop the "missionary zeal" of career foreign service officials towards South Africa. Kissinger would soon fulfil his promise in Easum's case. Easum himself provided Kissinger the proverbial last straw on the camel's back with his statements during the African tour. At Dar es Salaam on November 2, 1974, Easum stated that the United States was using its influence to foster changes in South Africa–not to preserve the status quo. On arriving at Lusaka the same day, he indicated that the United States would keep its options open regarding the issue of South Africa's membership in the United Nations. He said that the expulsion issue would certainly arise in the General Assembly in the future and that the degree to which South Africa had made meaningful changes would determine the stances countries would take on such occasions. The next day Easum, while responding to press enquiries, stated that it was the American policy to deny visas for high ranking South African military officials to visit the United States unless the visit was for purely private purposes.

Easum's statements infuriated Kissinger, for this was not the time to provoke the South Africans. Kissinger believed that the position held by the Department of States' Bureau of African Affairs in the past decade had been in support of the Black African view of South Africa, one which took a "blind eye approach" to growing Soviet and Cuban involvement in Africa (Bissel, 1982, p.27). This position had to be reversed and the representatives of such attitudes like Easum had to be purged. In Easum's place was appointed Nathaniel Davis, who was ambassador to Chile at the time Allende's government was overthrown. Kissinger preferred Davis as he felt that the latter would take a less pro-Black approach. Moreover, the appointment was meant to be a signal to South Africa that the United States would not support any drastic change in policy towards it. Close on the heels of the appointment came reports that the United States would provide South Africa with enriched uranium for its first big nuclear power plant (Wilson, 1975).

The War of Words

While Kissinger was making plans to befriend South Africa, a verbal battle was taking place at the United Nations. The episode began in October 1975 when Clarence Mitchell of the National Association for the Advancement of Colored People (NAACP) and a member of the American delegation to the United Nations, addressed the Special Committee of the Security Council where he declared that apartheid was an odious and abhorrent system to which the United States had stated its opposition in numerous debates in successive sessions of the General Assembly. In the General Assembly Mitchell repeated his barrage of criticism of apartheid. He reiterated that the policy of the United States government was to encourage peaceful change in South Africa, from policies of apartheid to policies which would provide for the attainment of basic human rights to all citizens regardless of race. Mitchell in particular stated that the United States deplored the detention of people whose only act was outspoken opposition to apartheid and that the South African government was "courting disaster" by using repressive measures which had the effect of closing all avenues for peaceful change (Mitchell, 1975, p.935).

Mitchell's speech stirred up a controversy in South Africa with Prime Minister B. J. Vorster objecting to the charge that people were being detained for their opposition to apartheid. By the end of November 1975, Mitchell was back in the United Nations to substantiate his charges with a six thousand word reply, containing a long list of persons in South African detention for opposing apartheid. Mitchell was critical of the South African legal system where laws made political opposition a crime. Such a thing was not regarded criminal elsewhere in the world. He pointed out that what was regarded legal in South Africa was illegal by the standards of a liberal society. Daniel Patrick Moynihan, the Ambassador to the United Nations stated that his country had introduced a totally new method of argument in the General Assembly, the equivalent of which was the "Brandeis brief" in the American legal system. Moynihan was critical of those countries which blamed the United States for its position on South Africa and regretted that no one cared or listened when the United States spoke against apartheid (Moynihan, 1979, pp.242-244).

Kissinger's grand strategy of trying to influence events in Southern Africa through counterinsurgency had suffered a setback because of congressional initiatives and activism. The significant interests that the United States had could not be abandoned because of this. A different route to the solution of problems had to be explored. Something had to be done about Rhodesia, Namibia and South Africa. Kissinger decided to take greater involvement as well as invest his personal prestige in finding solutions because of his concern for instability and its consequences. By now it looked more certain than ever that Black nationalist movements would win the war against White regimes. It also seemed probable that the crisis in Southern Africa would threaten the interests of western capital and help the Soviet Union in its objectives. Until then, American policymakers had held the belief that South Africa was virtually impregnable and capable of withstanding any combination of internal and external threats. This belief began to erode as White regimes were being threatened more and more by increasing African discontent and by enhanced political and military support for guerrillas operating from Angola and Mozambique. The United States was apprehensive of the radicalisation of nationalist movements particularly in Rhodesia. The greatest threat this could ultimately pose was to South Africa where the United States had considerable interests. Therefore, to maintain the status quo in South Africa, peaceful and controlled transition of power, with moderate African leadership assuming power, became necessary. As the United States viewed it, the greatest beneficiary of such change was the White regime in South Africa. For several years South Africa had been assisting Rhodesia in withstanding international sanctions. But by now Rhodesia was a millstone around South Africa's neck. Ian Smith's obduracy was inviting the spread of Communism. Rhodesia was also an issue interfering with South Africa's efforts to normalise relations with other African countries. Since both the United States and South Africa had common and specific interests in this regard, it became possible for the former to communicate the message to the latter.

Shuttle Diplomacy in Southern Africa

Kissinger's name has already gone into history books in association with "shuttle diplomacy". In 1976 he applied it to Southern Africa. Kissinger recognised the need for majority rule in Rhodesia and the role that South Africa could play in making it a reality. Since his reputation had been stained in the debacles of Vietnam and Angola, he also needed to restore his image. It was ironic indeed that South Africa was to apprise Rhodesia of the virtues of majority rule when the South African minority itself did not believe in the principle. Personally Kissinger felt that Southern Africa was a rural backwater which needed a taste of his intervention and style of diplomacy. As an aide of the British Prime Minister James Callaghan observed, it would have worked even though he went in for the wrong reasons (Martin and Johnson, 1981, p.233).

Rhodesia, in 1976 was in a crisis. The guerrilla war had intensified, spreading beyond its borders, creating strains on the economy and encouraging emigration. Despite all this, Smith was not prepared to give up power. Kissinger hoped to enlist South African support in persuading Smith to step down. The United States had planned a three step initiative for Southern Africa. Firstly, peace had to be made with Black Africans who were troubled about American collusion with South Africa in Angola. Secondly, the Frontline states had to be persuaded to accept some general terms for the peaceful transition of power in Rhodesia and Namibia. Thirdly, South Africa, after being apprised of these terms, had to take the initiative for a diplomatic settlement in Rhodesia and then in Namibia (Bissel, 1982, p.29).

Once he had done the groundwork in this connection, Kissinger prepared for his historic African safari. At a news conference on April 22, 1976, he stated that he would clarify during his visit what the American position with respect to South Africa would be, and would also extend the strong support of the United States for majority rule in Southern Africa. To a question whether he thought that majority rule in Rhodesia was possible in the next decade, he replied in the affirmative (Kissinger, 1976a, p.617). Kissinger's major pronouncement during the trip was his speech in Lusaka on April 27, 1976. He declared that his journey was intended to give fresh impetus to American co-operation and usher in a new era in United States policy. He did not want previous American policies to be raked up because nothing could be gained in a debate whether in the past the United States had neglected Africa or had been insufficiently committed to American goals. The United States had several responsibilities in the post war world and was not in a position to focus on all issues at the same time. Kissinger went to the extent of hailing the Lusaka Manifesto of 1969 and comparing it to the American Declaration of Independence. He proceeded with a ten point programme for Rhodesia. The centrepiece of Kissinger's speech was:

> The United States will continue to encourage and work for peaceful change. Our policy toward South Africa is based upon the premise that within a reasonable time we shall see a clear evolution toward equality of opportunity and basic human rights for all South Africans. (Kissinger, 1976b, pp.672-679)

Equally significant was Kissinger's call on South Africa to show its dedication to Africa by using its influence in Rhodesia to promote a rapid negotiated settlement for majority rule. *The Times* wrote that it was probably the most important statement of policy on Africa ever made by an American leader. It pointed out, however, that Kissinger was not very specific about American policy towards South Africa, except to state that his government would continue to encourage and work for peaceful change there. With some sarcasm, perhaps, it observed that Kissinger's comparison of the Lusaka Manifesto to the Declaration of Independence was no doubt to establish the United States as another "revolutionary brother".[6] *The Guardian* was not so optimistic about the Kissinger mission. It could not see Kissinger as the person most likely to solve the problems of Southern Africa and expressed doubts whether the South African government would enforce sanctions against Rhodesia and risk the anger of its largely pro-Rhodesian White electorate.[7]

Black Africa was listening to Kissinger, but many there did not take his rhetoric seriously. Setting foot on Africa after almost a decade, Kissinger tried hard to portray his policy as a humanitarian concern for peaceful change in the region. To his critics, it did not sound convincing enough. Julius Nyerere, President of Tanzania, readily brushed aside Kissinger's ethically coated verbosity. With scepticism, he remarked that racially oppressive situations had existed for a long time in Southern Africa, but there never had been any convincing evidence of American concern in mitigating them (Jackson, 1982, p.275). On the other hand, some observers felt that the Presidents of the Frontline states reacted favourably to Kissinger's statements, because the support for majority rule coming from the United States after several years of tilt in the other direction was undoubtedly gratifying (Legum, 1976, p.761).

The American effort was meant to bring change in Southern Africa except South Africa. The fate of South Africa was something that Kissinger did not want to discuss. Senator Dick Clark remarked that the South African situation was not a problem to be addressed after the situations in Rhodesia and Namibia had been resolved. He felt that the South African situation posed the greatest threat of widespread racial violence and massive foreign intervention in Southern Africa. He pointed out that if the United States was serious about its new policy it would have to address the South Africa policy squarely, using all possible means to avert confrontation.[8] The Ford administration saw no reason to tamper with the South African apartheid regime which appeared relatively stable and which protected American interests. Kissinger's entire rhetoric on majority rule was meant to abandon the Smith regime, while supporting the Vorster regime. Upon reflection, Kissinger's Lusaka speech was merely a recognition of changes in the status quo which preceded its delivery. Basically the premise of Option Two remained undisturbed in the case of South Africa. The speech "sought to forestall fundamental changes (i.e., revolutionary) by advocating gradualism–at the expense of a very unpopular Smith regime in Rhodesia". At no point did Kissinger extend the "logic of the proposed positions" to South Africa (Leighton, 1976, pp.17-18). In essence, the speech was a message to the South African government that the United States would give it time to enact a moderate programme of economic and social reform in exchange for co-operation on Rhodesia.

Although the speech was made in the midst of a Black African audience, the message was meant for South Africa. Prime Minister B. J. Vorster had by now realised the futility of continued support for

Rhodesia. He was reluctantly preparing to withdraw South Africa from its outer defences of Rhodesia, if not Namibia, in return for Black recognition of White rule in South Africa. In the new circumstances, a moderate Black African government, like the one in Botswana, was preferable in Rhodesia to a White regime. Moreover, the economic situation in South Africa demanded a more realistic foreign policy. Gold sales by the United States, though initially beneficial to South Africa, had brought down its price to $126 an ounce, with indications that it would further slide to $80. South Africa was at that time searching for international credit to finance arms and petroleum purchases. At the diplomatic level, an accommodation with the United States was becoming necessary. This would confer unprecedented recognition on the South African regime. It would also bring the regime legitimacy and above all stall moves for majority rule in South Africa. The differences that South Africa had with Rhodesia were on the increase while on several issues South African interests converged with those of the United States. While South Africa had been thoroughly integrated into the international economic system, Rhodesia was not. Rhodesian Whites were becoming a liability for South Africa. The ultimate attempt of the West was therefore to create in Rhodesia a Black regime that would keep the country within a South African dominated economic system (Leighton, 1976, p.24).

Vorster's initial reaction to Kissinger's African trip and the accompanying pronouncements was guarded. He stated that in view of the fact that Kissinger made announcements and prescribed solutions without consulting Southern African countries including South Africa, it was difficult to make an assessment of American policy. Kissinger, Vorster said, was putting the United States on a "no win course because in fact he is now sitting down to sup with the devil and he should know that his spoon isn't long enough to do that". Vorster felt that Kissinger had made superficial platitudes in his Lusaka speech and had not satisfied anybody.[9]

Meanwhile, in the United States, Kissinger's "new" Africa policy evoked responses from several quarters. Before embarking on his African mission, Kissinger had made efforts to enlist support from the influential centres of power. Republican Congressmen like Senator Charles Percy and prominent Democrats like George McGovern were kept sufficiently informed of his moves. But while taking care of his left flank, Kissinger ignored the right flank within the Republican party, particularly presidential aspirants like Ronald Reagan who were critical of the administration's foreign policy. Addressing the Senate Foreign Relations Committee on May 13, 1976, Kissinger had said that President Ford planned to follow up actively on

American pledges of moral, political and economic support for Black nationalist movements in South Africa. Kissinger told the panel that the United States had regained the initiative in Southern Africa and that several African leaders had agreed that outside powers should not deal directly in future with the liberation movements of the region.[10] Kissinger however, sounded more zealous than those African leaders themselves. Conservatives in the United States, criticising Kissinger, said that the American pledges of support for Black nationalist movements were made without consulting Congress. Senator James B. Allen declared that he took strong exception to Kissinger's Africa policy which would reward nations in Africa seeking to topple one of the two or three stable regimes, namely Rhodesia, in the entire continent of chaos.[11]

Kissinger maintained that by offering a realistic alternative to violent change, the possibilities had been enhanced for Blacks and Whites to work out for themselves the mode of their future existence and co-operation. South Africa, he said, was being offered the opportunity to turn away from its increasingly isolated position and positively engage in a modest and hopeful process of peaceful change (Kissinger, 1976c, p.717). Observers of American policy were closely watching the increased involvement of the United States in Southern Africa. They believed that Kissinger was viewing South Africa as the "main lever" to influence the Rhodesian regime. They were almost certain that South Africa would begin using coercive measures if Rhodesia failed to change. But at the same time they wondered what price the South Africans would demand in terms of American support.[12]

Soweto and the Meetings in Europe

By mid May 1976, Kissinger had also been negotiating with South Africa's ambassador in Washington, R. F. (Pik) Botha. Kissinger made it clear to him that the primary responsibility of persuading Smith to agree to a transfer of power in Rhodesia would be that of South Africa. As preliminary talks went on, in June it was announced that Kissinger would meet Vorster in Bavaria later that month. As Fine (1977, p.23) comments, Kissinger had concluded that it would require an American Secretary of State to discharge with honour Britain's last imperial responsibility in Africa. But this "assignment was tactical, it did not call for the explication of principles or the elaboration of a new direction".

As preparations for the meeting in Bavaria were going on, violence broke out in South Africa. Although there were several Black grievances already in existence, the immediate provocation was the government decision to introduce Afrikaans as a medium of instruction in schools. This was widely resented and the protest culminated in violence in the Soweto township where about seventy people were killed in police firing. The events had a tremendous impact in the United States, especially as talks with South Africa were just about to begin. For Afro-Americans particularly, what appeared in the media regarding events in the land of their ancestors was appalling. The administration was on its guard because it knew that there would be widespread condemnation of the apartheid regime. Soweto provided American policymakers with several lessons. Such incidents could rebound on American national interests, intensify racial antagonism within the United States and even provide the catalyst for Afro-American dissent in the armed forces, if not mutiny (Jackson, 1982, p.246). Soweto made it clear that it was no longer merely a question of American strategic theories or corporate interests in South Africa. It was an issue of race, and the repercussions of racial strife could permeate American society. The violence at Soweto made Kissinger's meeting with Vorster even more delicate than ever before. Nevertheless, it was decided to hold the Bavarian meeting as planned. On the eve of his departure, Kissinger admitted that he regretted the events and went out of his way to assure Congressmen that he would raise the issue of human rights during the talks.[13] The African media expressed surprise at the fact that Kissinger did not recoil at the prospect of sitting at the same table as Vorster, when racial violence was at its height in South Africa.[14]

When Kissinger and Vorster met in Bavaria in June 1976, it was the first time since 1948 that such a high level American official was meeting a South African Prime Minister. On the one hand the meeting was an acknowledgement by the United States of South Africa's significance, particularly of its key role in Southern Africa. On the other hand it showed that the United States objectives in Rhodesia coincided with those of South Africa. Although no details about the talks were given, Kissinger made it known that their discussions started from the assumption that South Africa was willing to help in working towards a peaceful solution. In a report to Congress following his meeting, Kissinger said that the prospects for negotiated settlements in Rhodesia and Namibia were enhanced. Time was running out and formidable barriers remained. He believed that if continued responsible efforts were made by all sides, the questions of South Africa could be solved without great loss of life, suffering and bitterness (Kissinger, 1976d, pp.47-48). In an address to the National Urban League, Kissinger appealed to South Africa to realise that the wind of change was blowing through Africa and that apartheid was a mockery of any definition of human equality. He promised that the United States, true to its own beliefs, would use all its influence to encourage peaceful change, equality of opportunity and basic human rights in South Africa.[15] Kissinger also thought that American policy was finding widespread support around the world and that this was the best chance for peaceful solutions and for a secure and just future for Africa, free from outside intervention (Kissinger, 1976e, p.262).

The meeting between Kissinger and Vorster in Bavaria was soon followed by another one in Zurich from September 4 to 6, 1976. In the interlude, South Africa had communicated to the Rhodesian White minority government that it was futile to remain in power. At the end of the Zurich meeting, Vorster publicly announced his acceptance of the principle of majority rule in Rhodesia. What promises he received from Kissinger in return were not revealed, but it looked almost certain that they included financial assurances, direct or indirect, and a promise of a more sympathetic American attitude towards South Africa in the United Nations. At a news conference in Zurich on September 6, Kissinger said that the United States was making a serious effort to achieve the objectives of majority rule and minority rights. It also sought a peaceful end to disagreements, and negotiations that would enable all communities to live under conditions of dignity and progress (Kissinger, 1976f, p.377). For Kissinger, the United States had to be true to its own beliefs. South Africa, he urged had to take account of the conscience of humanity. "Our policy", he said, "is based upon the premise that within a reasonable period of time we shall see a clear evolution toward just internal arrangements" (Kissinger, 1976g, p.354).

The Last Phase of Kissinger's African Safari

In mid September, Kissinger set out again on another of his historic voyages to Africa, for talks on the political future of the Whites in Southern Africa. In South Africa he had two days of discussions with Vorster and also met with Black Africans. Later Kissinger met Ian Smith to persuade him to agree to the American-South African plan. His message was reinforced separately by Vorster. The expected bombshell came on September 24 when Smith announced that he had accepted Kissinger's terms which appeared to concede to a handover of power to a Black African government in Rhodesia within two years. On the same day President Ford welcomed the announcement and promised full support to all the parties involved (Ford, 1976, p.528). The world was surprised by what seemed to be a complete "about turn" by Smith. The "formidable combination of carrot and stick" administered by Kissinger and Vorster appeared effective where the efforts of Harold Wilson and his negotiators had failed (Tinker, 1977, p.128). The threat of South Africa to impede the flow of imports and exports to Rhodesia had made an impact. However, what was perceived to be a foreign policy success for Kissinger was to some Black African leaders an act of the United States to contain Soviet influence rather than a sincere commitment to the concept of majority rule (Darnston, 1976).

Kissinger wanted to utilise this success in the presidential elections in the United States scheduled for November 1976. By the end of October the Geneva negotiations on Rhodesia had commenced and still continued at the time of the elections. There was a widespread belief that the American concentration on Rhodesia was to divert attention from the problems of South Africa itself. The administration tried to assure critics that efforts in Rhodesia would not dilute the American capacity to influence favourably developments in South Africa. It stated that, on the contrary, if war in those neighbouring areas could be avoided and the thrust shifted from violence to negotiations as the way to resolve racial conflict, the United States would have a profoundly positive effect on the circumstances within South Africa. The United States was aware of the economic and strategic importance of South Africa. The administration believed, that it was important for American business to continue to reflect the principles of the United States in their operations in South Africa. This, it believed, could be done despite the existence of institutionalised discrimination against Blacks (Rogers, 1976, pp.533-536).

In the Presidential elections of November 1976 Ford was defeated by the Democratic candidate Jimmy Carter. Soon after this the Geneva negotiations on Rhodesia collapsed. Kissinger had given the impression to both sides in Rhodesia and the Frontline states that the other party had agreed to their conditions. His scheme was eventually exposed as an ambiguous effort, one that failed to bring about a genuine agreement. Each side withdrew from the negotiations for its own reasons. South Africa also withdrew support for the Kissinger deal. Moreover, by now South Africa had become less interested in responding to outside initiatives. It was more concerned about developments within the country arising out of Soweto.

Bissel (1982, p.31) writes that "even though Kissinger had negotiated a package deal of responsible satisfaction to the South Africans, the departure of the Ford administration and the internal problems of South Africa ensured the cancelling of that deal".

Transkei

The question regarding the recognition of Transkei was a South African issue that the Ford administration had to deal with during its last days. Transkei was one of the homelands created by South Africa and was given the right to govern itself. On October 26, 1976 South Africa declared Transkei independent. On September 21, a little more than a month before this, the United States House of Representatives rejected a resolution calling upon the administration to recognise the new state. Supporters of the resolution like Philip M. Crane and Larry P. McDonald declared that the rejection of Transkei was the rejection of a Black nation which had sought independence through diplomatic negotiations and peaceful means. They charged that it was the height of hypocrisy not to extend recognition to Transkei because of South Africa's social policies when the United States was recognising nations like the Soviet Union and Communist China. Opponents of the resolution including Stephen J. Solarz, on the other hand argued that the United States should reject the policy of apartheid. Solarz thought that the rejection of the resolution would deter Kissinger from recognising Transkei in return for South African assistance on Rhodesia.[16]

Later that year when the United Nations General Assembly voted not to recognise Transkei, the United States abstained. Justifying the American position at a news conference in Hartford, Connecticut, Kissinger (1976h, p.643) stated that the difficulty with the resolution was that it contained an acceptable part as well as an unacceptable one. The United States was prepared to accept the one that called for the non-recognition of Transkei but not the one which urged members not to have any dealings with anybody in Transkei. The United States, he said, would continue to deal with Transkei as if it were part of South Africa. It could not accept the proposition that one could not deal with the people of Transkei just because South Africa had declared it an independent state. The American objection, Kissinger maintained, was a technical one. If that part had been removed, the United States would have voted for it.

Long before these developments, experts on Southern African affairs had stated that, on questions of difficult choice like recognition or extension of economic or educational assistance to independent homelands, the United States had to be guided by the collective judgement of African states as expressed through the Organisation of African Unity. American credibility was a scarce and vital resource. But if it was used in the way it had been previously, as in the case of dealing with the Portuguese and South African regimes, it would only undermine further the creative potential of American policy (Marcum, 1976, p.424).

Kissinger did not have any concrete programme for change in South Africa. His strategy was to align more closely with Vorster and to secure agreements in Rhodesia and Namibia and also gain time for the South African government to reform its own system. Whether it reformed or not did not seem to be a concern for Kissinger. The Kissinger mission to Southern Africa was projected as a humanitarian one, while in reality there was nothing altruistic about it. Julius Nyerere (1977a, pp.672-673) wrote in *Foreign Affairs*:

> The 'Kissinger initiative' did force Ian Smith to shift his ground, but it did not succeed in its declared objective. Neither did it remove Africa's uncertainty about the depth and geographical limitations of America's new commitment to change in southern Africa. For decades of history cannot be wiped out by one speech and a few months of highly individualistic one-man diplomacy.

It was still not clear whether the United States had committed itself to majority rule in Africa as a universal principle or as a solution just for Rhodesia. Kissinger had carefully avoided any reference to the subject of majority rule in South Africa itself. Many Africans had the suspicion that this was the price Kissinger paid Vorster for the latter's role in "converting Smith". For Africans this had to be stated clearly because the moral position of majority rule was viewed by them as absolute. Critics of American policy towards Africa did not find much to praise. To achieve immediate gains, Kissinger must have compromised on other matters. Never did Kissinger's approach deviate from the concerns of realpolitik. George Ball, a former American Under Secretary of State, described the whole issue as an episode in which the United States tried to gloss over inherently unstable situations in order to show immediate results (Ball, 1976, pp.20-22).

If all these represented the sum total of compromises of principles, why was a great effort made by the United States in getting involved in the crisis situations in Southern Africa? It can be concluded that the Soviet penetration into Southern Africa was the major reason for greater involvement in the affairs of the region. For several years American "benign neglect" characterised policy towards Africa. Interest skyrocketed only when Soviet backed regimes took over in Angola and Mozambique and further threatened American interests in Southern Africa. Fearing that a racial war in Rhodesia, Namibia and South Africa would bring the entire region under Soviet domination and strengthen global polarisation, the United States jumped in to defuse the powder keg. Moreover, Washington was worried that a racial war in Africa would reopen the wounds of racial confrontation in the United States itself, where they were beginning to heal. The Ford administration was not concerned about the problems in South Africa. It was more interested in promoting controlled change in Rhodesia and Namibia so that South Africa would be insulated from any radical changes in those countries.

The administration had intended to continue the policy of its predecessor. But Option Two which governed American policy for almost five years lost its significance in the wake of the Portuguese developments. The conviction dawned late that existing policy was not sufficient to handle situations which had the potential to develop into serious crises with grave implications for American foreign and domestic policy. By the time the United States felt the need to intervene in Southern Africa, the situation was one step ahead of policy and beyond American control.

Notes

1. *Angola* (1976), Hearings before the Subcommittee on Africa, Senate Committee on Foreign Relations, 94th Congress, Second Session, Government Printing Office, Washington, DC.
2. The Senate Intelligence Committee issued its year long study in mid 1978 documenting American collusion with South Africa.
3. The domino theory is the doctrine that states that if some key nation or geographical region falls under Communist control, a string of other nations will subsequently topple like a row of dominoes.
4. *Washington Post*, October 31, 1974.
5. "An Unwise UN Move", *Christian Science Monitor* (Boston) October 2, 1974.
6. *The Times* (London) April 28, 1976.
7. *The Guardian* (London) April 28, 1976.

8. "Probe Into US African Policy", *Congressional Quarterly Weekly Report* (Washington, DC) 34:27, July 3, 1976, p. 1713.
9. "John Vorster Reviews Africa's Race Conflict", Interview with John Vorster, *International Herald Tribune* (Paris) May 10, 1976.
10. "Secretary Kissinger's Address to the Senate Foreign Relations Committee", May 13, 1976, *Congressional Quarterly Weekly Report* (Washington, DC) 34:20, May 15, 1976, p. 1155.
11. "Conservatives Oppose New African Policy", *Congressional Quarterly Weekly Report* (Washington, DC) 34: 24, June 12, 1976, p. 1569.
12. *The Guardian* (London), June 5, 1976.
13. *The Guardian* (London), June 18, 1976.
14. *The Standard* (Nairobi), June 30, 1976.
15. *Times of India* (New Delhi), August 4, 1976.
16. "Independence for Transkei", *Congressional Quarterly Weekly Report* (Washington, DC) 34: 42, October 16, 1976, p. 3022.

6 Human Rights and Enlightened Capitalism: Agenda of the Carter Administration

Jimmy Carter's election to the White House raised high hopes in the minds of many who desired a change from the two preceding administrations, particularly regarding United States policy towards South Africa. To a great extent this impression was created as a result of Carter's background and the message he had conveyed during the election campaign. He spoke of moralism, human rights and also of the shortcomings of the previous Republican administrations. Carter was particularly critical of the administrations which he believed had evolved a kind of secretive "Lone Ranger" foreign policy–a one man policy of international adventure which was not appropriate for the United States. On East-West relations, he wanted the competition to be peaceful and co-operation to increase, but was opposed to any kind of accommodation which went against the interests of the United States and its allies. He saw the North-South conflict as part of a security problem and that insofar as American policy was selfish, cynical or short-sighted, there would inevitably be a day of reckoning (Carter, 1977a, pp.115-121). On social justice, human rights and the environment, Carter considered himself quite a liberal, while in the management of government, a conservative (Kucharsky, 1976, p.98). One could find most of these sentiments in Carter's Inaugural Address, in which he stated that the United States was a strong nation and that its strength was based not on the size of its arsenal but on the nobility of its ideas. Americans could never be indifferent to the fate of freedom elsewhere in the world because they were free. Carter said that the moral sense of Americans dictated a clear-cut preference for those societies which shared with them an abiding respect for individual human rights (Carter, 1977a, pp.253-256).

Carter's personal philosophy reflected in his statements on South Africa too and he was determined to put increased pressure on that country. As Senator Dick Clark put it, nowhere would a change in the administration be more welcome and nowhere was it needed more than with respect to the long term policy towards Africa. He wanted the new administration to start with a clean slate with none of the disastrous and deceptive policies of the Nixon-Ford-Kissinger years (Clark, 1977, pp.1-4). Carter's assumptions concerning South Africa reflected the views of the "New Politics" wing within the Democratic Party. "South Africa was Georgia writ large, and South Africa must be freed" (Duignan and Gann, 1984, p.294). One crucial factor which contributed to Carter's electoral victory was his emphasis on moral values and human rights.

Carter also emphasised the need for improved relations with the Soviet Union. The Soviet Union he believed, had limited aims in Africa and there was no need for a show of strength by the United States in this regard. Carter was concerned about American relations with African governments and the level of influence with them. On assumption of office, the Carter administration had a free hand with respect to policy towards Africa, apart from the fact that the programmes and decisions of the previous administration had influenced the agenda of the new one. The United States had already involved itself in the affairs of Southern Africa and there was no question of going back on it. It had to demonstrate a new approach to policymaking. While Kissinger had viewed the importance of American involvement in Southern Africa in global terms, the Carter administration considered it in regional terms. The Carter administration established an agenda of foreign policy goals in Africa that gave importance to the implementation of human rights. Such an agenda was perceived by many as directed against the White minority governments.

Human Rights

In essence, two major principles governed the administration's initial approach to African affairs. Firstly, the administration attempted to disconnect its behaviour in Africa from competitiveness with the Soviet Union. Secondly, the treatment of African affairs was placed within the broader interest of the administration in promoting higher standards of human rights through American foreign policy decisions. While the emphasis on human rights was global in its design, it was particularly applicable to Africa where White minority governments still existed. But several factors would decelerate the application of these principles. A new administration with a novel approach was not in a position to change things overnight in another part of the world. Furthermore, it was not certain what the response within the United States would be to any increased attention given to Southern Africa. Finally other domestic factors, and policies of other powers were also important in this regard (Bissel, 1977, p.156).

The appointments that Carter made reflected his priorities and also largely represented the McGovernite minority within the Democratic Party. Walter Mondale, who was Carter's running mate, played a special role in formulating general policy. Andrew Young, a prominent Afro-American became Ambassador to the United Nations and Anthony Lake, a specialist in African affairs took charge as Director of the Policy Planning Staff. Interestingly, Carter retained William Schaufele, Assistant Secretary of State for African Affairs, who had held that post in the previous administration. The views of the new appointees to a great extent corresponded with that of Carter. Perhaps the most important and controversial of all these men, particularly with regard to Africa policy was Andrew Young. He had behind him a career of leading the civil rights movement in the United States. An adherent of the "New Politics" wing, he viewed South Africa as a microcosm of the western world in its relations with the Third World. Young felt strongly that in the past the United States had sided with the world's tyrants. This evil had to be set right by applying the principles of the civil rights movement. African issues had to be treated through existing institutions especially the United Nations. As Ambassador to the United Nations, Young clearly had a leading role in developing policy towards Africa and had created good contacts with his African counterparts. "The issue (human rights), the spokesmen (Mr. Young and the President) and the target (South Africa) were all in position" (Uttley, 1979-1980, p.4).

The previous administration had bungled over the Rhodesian issue. Carter realised that bringing the nationalist movements fighting the White regime to the bargaining table required the co-operation of the leaders of the neighbouring Black ruled states from whom they were receiving military and diplomatic support. Those leaders could not be expected to co-operate unless they were convinced that the United States was not committed to perpetuating White supremacy in the region. The American bona fides therefore lay in the ability of the United States to apply pressure on South Africa to dismantle apartheid. It was also necessary to reassure African leaders that co-operation was worth the risk (Foltz, 1985, p.37).

For two months, until the end of March 1977, the policy towards South Africa was reviewed and debated. Schaufele, the inherited Assistant Secretary advocated continuation of the Kissinger policy of not putting pressure on South Africa. The counterargument articulated by Young and supported by Lake was that the Carter administration, to be true to what it represented not only had to take a resolute stand against South Africa but also had to be seen publicly doing so. They wanted the Africa policy to be detached from East-West considerations and the rejection of Kissinger's concept of linkage (Uttley, 1979-1980, p.4).

Policy Review Memorandum 4

Policy Review Memorandum 4 (PRM 4), prepared under the supervision of Zbigniew Brzezinski, the National Security Adviser, was the administration's substitute for the infamous NSSM 39. The authors of PRM 4 debated whether to maintain Kissinger's emphasis on pursuing settlements in Rhodesia and Namibia with South Africa's co-operation before directing attention on South Africa itself, or to confront South Africa immediately and directly without waiting for solutions elsewhere. The advocates of the second view led by Young prevailed upon Carter. Accordingly, in March 1977, Carter signed a confidential presidential directive to guide policy in Southern Africa. The directive emphasised that Southern African problems be regarded as urgent, and that the United States remain committed to peaceful solutions since guerrilla warfare could be exploited by the Soviet Union in its own interests. It also stated that the United States should work in co-operation with its European allies and African states to find solutions. With regard to South Africa, the directive stressed the need for the United States to take a stronger stand against apartheid or imperil its relations with the Third World. It also emphasised that steps be taken to scale down American relations with South Africa if the minority regime refused to consider sharing power with the Blacks. In Goldsworthy's words, "selective relaxation was out, selective hardening was in" (Goldsworthy, 1980, pp.228-229).

The new premise arrived at by the administration was that it was in South Africa's own interest to help resolve the problems of Rhodesia and Namibia and that there was no need for the United States to seek an accommodation with Pretoria. This argument was considered important because the new goal of overall Africa policy was to strengthen American standing among Black African states in order to assure them of United States' support. The administration repudiated the agreement concluded between Kissinger and Smith over Rhodesia and refused to accord recognition to the moderate and racially mixed government in Salisbury. In the case of South Africa, it dropped the Kissinger policy of limited and quiet co-operation. The administration wanted to make it clear that its policy was different from that of the previous one. The acceptance of the new policy led to William Schaufele's resignation and the appointment of Richard Moose as the Assistant Secretary of State for African Affairs.

South Africa remained cautious of the new administration and its policies. Even as early as the American presidential election day in November 1976, when asked if he was worried about Carter, the South African Prime Minister Vorster replied that it was "more a question of wondering rather than worrying" (Bissel, 1982, p.31). However, the South Africans were almost certain that they had to expect a different approach from the Carter administration.

The Vienna Meeting

The Carter administration made it clear that it was serious about South Africa when in May 1977, Vice President Walter Mondale flew to Vienna for a meeting with Vorster. *The Sunday Times* stated in anticipation, that Mondale would make clear that President Carter's whole outlook was governed by the prospects of Black majority rule throughout the region. It also pointed out that the new American policy was influenced not only by Carter's attitude to human rights but also the American experience with its own civil rights movement.[1] At Vienna, Mondale officially warned South Africa to dismantle apartheid or suffer deterioration in its relations with the United States. On June 20, after his meeting with Vorster, he stated at a press conference that there was need for progress on all three issues: majority rule for Rhodesia and Namibia; and a "progressive transformation of South African society to the same end". The United States, he said, could not accept let alone defend the governments that rejected the basic principle of full human rights, economic opportunity and political participation for all its people regardless of race. He further stated:

> On the issue of South African policies, it is our position that separateness and apartheid are inherently discriminatory and that that policy of apartheid cannot be acceptable to us. We also are of the opinion strongly held that full political participation by all the citizens of South Africa–equal participation in the elections of its national government and its

political affairs–is essential to a healthy, stable and secure South Africa. (Mondale, 1977, pp.661-663)

Mondale was asked by journalists to elaborate on the concept of full participation as opposed to "one man, one vote". When asked whether there was any kind of compromise in this regard, Mondale affirmed that "every citizen should have the right to vote and every vote should be equally weighted".[2] Mondale had made clear what exactly the administration meant and that was exactly what South Africa needed to justify adopting an uncompromising stand. To the Whites, the concept of "one man one vote" was unacceptable. They considered it a portent of their destruction. Mondale's open announcement at Vienna eventually led to their intransigence (Pogrund, 1977, p.58). South African sources said that Vorster was not prepared to yield to American demands for major changes in his government's racial segregation policies and that he was reconciled to the inevitable deterioration of relations with the United States and its allies.[3] *The International Herald Tribune* stated that full participation meant broadly that all Blacks would participate in the political system within a unitary South African state, not just within Black homelands. It also said that "one man, one vote" was a phrase open to the interpretation that Washington was seeking "to apply to South Africa's differing circumstances the fully democratic pattern in effect in the United States".[4] Donald F. McHenry, Young's deputy at the United Nations pointed out that Mondale's task was to deliver the South Africans a twofold message. The first was that progress had to be made on each of the three issues of Rhodesia, Namibia and South Africa. The second was related to South Africa itself, that unless there was an end to racial discrimination, and progress towards full political participation, the United States would have to review and change its policies towards South Africa (McHenry, 1978, p.36).

The Carter administration wanted the United States to align with progressive forces and persuade South Africa to bring about racial equality and integration through gradual reform. It was considered that it would require both persistence and patience to carry on the dialogue just started. However, there had to be a certain amount of caution while pursuing the new policy. There was always the possibility of intransigent South African Whites retreating into isolation, or to use their own old expression, to "laager up".[5]

The Administration Speaks Out

Around the time Mondale was in Vienna, Young was in Maputo attending a United Nations Conference on Southern Africa, where he assured Black Africa and leaders like Robert Mugabe and Sam Nujoma that the United States was on their side and that unlike previous occasions this time it really meant business. Addressing the conference, Young pointed out that at the heart of tensions in Southern Africa was the smouldering racial crisis in South Africa itself. He asserted that American policies reflected the commitment to human rights and that change had to begin immediately in South Africa (Young, 1977, pp.55-59). Young's credentials as a noted civil rights leader gave him privileged access to Black leaders, but the policy he advocated was treated with "prudent scepticism" (Uttley, 1979-1980, p.5). During his Southern African trip, Young also wanted to visit South Africa. But the South African government said that it would not be convenient for them to receive him as he also intented to meet Black leaders. Young had already entered their bad books because in April 1977 he had replied in the affirmative to an interviewer on being asked whether he considered South Africa's minority government "illegitimate". The South Africans had demanded a clarification and the Secretary of State Cyrus Vance told Young that he had misstated American policy. Young replied that his usage "illegitimate" could be interpreted "morally, ethically or legally" and that he considered the South African government "unrepresentative of its people, but still the agency in charge in the country".[6]

Until then it looked as though Carter was leaving to the members of his administration the responsibility to speak on Southern Africa. Carter's pronouncements came in his famous speech made at the commencement of the Notre Dame University on May 22, 1977. He made it clear that the United States' commitment to majority rule applied to South Africa no less than to other countries in the region. The United States was committed to a peaceful resolution of the crisis in Southern Africa. Carter stated that the time had come "for the principle of majority rule to be the basis for political order, recognising that in a democratic system the rights of the minority" also had to be protected (Carter, 1977b, p.961). In an interview with the Magazine Publishers Association, Carter said that the United States did not feel inclined to intrude into South Africa's internal policies but was committed to having equality of treatment of citizens. The United States, he said, was not trying to overthrow the South African government but felt that there ought to be some equality in that country (Carter, 1977b, pp.1089-1090).

Another major announcement regarding the administration's policy was made by Secretary of State Cyrus Vance while addressing a meeting of the National Association for the Advancement of Colored People (NAACP). He emphasised the administration's human rights policy as far as Southern Africa was concerned. American policies, he said, had to reflect American values. The deep belief in human rights meant making the best effort peacefully in promoting racial justice in the countries of Southern Africa. He also went on to say that the most effective policies towards Africa were affirmative policies which were not to be reactive to the deeds of other powers or to each crisis as it arose. A negative, reactive American policy which only sought to oppose Soviet or Cuban involvement in Africa was both dangerous and futile. There was a need to recognise the importance of economic development and indigenous nationalism to African states. The United States had to give greater importance to economic co-operation and active diplomacy. At the same time military links and arms sales had to be downplayed, he said (Vance, 1977a, pp.310-319). Vance's speech was considered important at that time because it was the first full length exposition of the administration's Africa policy.[7]

The first half of 1977 thus saw a barrage of speeches by Carter and his associates on Southern Africa. Reactions to the speeches were also to follow. For instance, George Ball pointed out that Mondale's Vienna statement had "created dismay in South Africa, confounding liberal opinion and strengthening the arguments of the obscurantists". He regarded Vance's speech as an effort to mitigate the damage already done. Ball felt that the inability of the political leaders to face the realities of the South African scene suggested "an ethnocentricity derived more from inexperience than presumption". The lessons of the American civil rights movement could not be applied to the South African case and the American ability to influence South African policies depended on the objectives the United States was seeking to achieve. He warned that "diplomacy like politics is the art of the possible; and if we use our leverage toward an unachievable end, we will create a mess" (Ball, 1977, pp.43-51).

Anti-Americanism had by this time become a powerful force in White South African politics. In an election held some months after his showdown with Mondale, Vorster was able to increase his majority in parliament by fifteen seats, just by focusing the electorate's attention on alleged American meddling in the country's affairs. South African statements during this period reflected an anti-American feeling. Carter's stance promoted a climate of distrust and he refused to acknowledge and endorse South Africa's dominant status in Southern Africa. This contributed to the increased steadfastness of the South African military to demonstrate the country's hegemony by destabilising the governments and economies of neighbouring states. The Carter administration on its part emphasised more and more the differences between the United States and South Africa.

The Sullivan Initiative

The human rights theme of the Carter administration had an impact on interest groups and American multinational corporations. In March 1977, a delegation consisting of representatives of eleven major American companies met Cyrus Vance to discuss South African issues. The delegation also included Reverend Leon Sullivan, an Afro-American pastor and member of the Board of Directors of General Motors. The outcome of the meeting was the decision to issue guidelines for American business operations in South Africa. An expanded version of the original six principles was published by Rev. Sullivan and was thereafter known as the Sullivan Principles or the Sullivan Code. The principles called for fairer and more favourable treatment of the Blacks who worked for American owned firms in South Africa. They called for the desegregation of all eating, comfort and work facilities; equal and fair employment practices, including support for the elimination of discrimination against the rights of the Blacks to form or belong to government registered trade unions; equal pay for comparable work and equitable wages well above the appropriate local minimum economic living level; the development of training programmes; the advancement of Blacks into managerial positions; and the improvement of the quality of employees' lives outside the work environment, including housing, transportation, schooling, recreation and health facilities.

Many American businesses with operations in South Africa adopted the Sullivan Principles, admitting that their managers were not particularly wedded to the conditions of work established by rigid apartheid. Those firms with large investments such as the automobile manufacturers who had a stake in expanding their sales to the Blacks were among the first to accept them. From the beginning, the administration gave strong support to the principles and in its statements urged American business in South Africa to adopt them wholeheartedly and to accept effective monitoring and reporting procedures. In a comprehensive public statement on United States economic policy, Assistant Secretary Moose observed that the Sullivan initiative sprang from the private corporate world and that it brought together American companies "voluntarily to pursue a common objective" and that this could be expected to survive a change in administrations (*South Africa: Time Running Out*, 1981, p.362). Critics argued that the principles became a rationale for foreign firms to continue their role in South Africa and that this only strengthened the White minority government. It was pointed out that the codes of conduct were being used by foreign companies as a justification for continued operations in South Africa. George Houser, Executive Director of the American Committee on Africa said that this was further testimony to the centrality of the issue of investment in South Africa (Houser, 1982, pp.23-29).

The results of the experiment were initially encouraging. A number of signatory companies tore down walls, removed signboards and shifted cabinets. Companies like Goodyear and Ford spent millions of dollars for the replacement of existing separate facilities with desegregated ones. Union Carbide, IBM and Caterpillar Tractor initiated housing loan programmes for Blacks. In areas like training and job advancement, limited but measurable progress was made by some firms. In the sphere of worker representation Blacks made gains. Ford and Kellogg recognised unregistered Black trade unions. A United Nations report of 1978, on the activities of transnational corporations in Southern Africa, referring to the Sullivan Principles stated that it was premature to judge the long term effect of "this corporate statement of social responsibility", especially since there were no specific criteria to make the principles operational.[8] Rev. Sullivan himself, in May 1980, while taking stock of the progress stated:

> I must caution again though that we realize how much the principles can and cannot accomplish. The principles are a catalyst. They can help produce change, but they cannot end apartheid by themselves. The principles can be a part of the solution, but by no means the whole solution, for in order to totally eliminate apartheid, help must come from the churches, unions, educational institutions, governments and world-wide opinion. (*United States Policy Toward South Africa,* 1980, p.347)

At the time of Rev. Sullivan's testimony only 135 out of about 350 American firms had endorsed the principles. There were several drawbacks associated with its application. For instance it was not easy to make an accurate assessment of the progress made. Disclosure policies of firms varied and some companies neither filed reports with Rev. Sullivan's group nor preferred to make them publicly available (*United States Policy Toward South Africa*, 1980, p.368). An observer stated that the negative aspect of the Sullivan Code was that it was being used as a Potemkin village to hide the ugly reality of a society built on White supremacy. He also said that on its own terms, the code was of extremely limited scope. It was only voluntary and even if made compulsory would apply to only less than 1 per cent of the American work force (*United States Policy Toward South Africa*, 1980, p.606). These were also more or less the arguments of a public statement issued by some prominent scholars and public personalities.[9]

Nuclear Impasse

South Africa's nuclear programme caused concern in the United States in 1977 when it was revealed that a Soviet satellite had photographed installations in the Kalahari desert, alleged to be a nuclear explosion test site. Carter ordered confirmation of the information. The Soviet information was proved to be correct. At the same time South Africa issued a series of categorical denials that any explosion was contemplated. Within the country there was a public outcry regarding the manner in which the United States was treating South Africa. However, the latter informed the United States that it did not intend developing nuclear explosive devices either for peaceful purposes or for a weapons programme. Carter was concerned about the ambivalence of the South African position. On the one hand Vorster had made a statement that South Africa had not given the United States assurances against the testing of atomic weapons. On the other hand as Carter stated, "in both a public statement that we've made and also in private dispatches through diplomatic channels and a private message directed to me from Vorster, they had unequivocally committed themselves not to design, nor produce, nor to test any atomic explosions at all, either peaceful or weapons" (Carter, 1977b, pp.1922-1923).

The United States continued to monitor the situation very closely and renewed efforts to encourage South Africa to place all its nuclear power production capabilities under international safeguards as well as to sign the Nuclear Nonproliferation Treaty (NPT). Carter welcomed South African assurances that it did not intend to explode nuclear devices despite the information provided by American intelligence sources. It should be noted that Vorster had denied that his statement was in reality a promise (Lockwood, 1977, p.14). Proposals by the Africanists in the Department of State to end all co-operation with South Africa in the nuclear field were vigorously opposed by the "liberals" in the Arms Control and Disarmament Agency and other regional bureaus. They argued that such an action would provoke South Africa into conducting a nuclear explosion and would undermine American nuclear nonproliferation efforts (Foltz, 1985, p.36). At one point, in a departure from the previous policy of only requiring comprehensive safeguards as a condition for nuclear exports, Carter stated that South Africa would have to sign the NPT in return for enriched uranium. Ambassador Gerard Smith, Carter's Special Representative for Nonproliferation matters, was sent to Pretoria in 1978 to persuade South Africa to sign the NPT. South Africa, however, not only wanted enriched uranium and components for its enrichment plant but also demanded American support in being reinstated in the International Atomic Energy Agency's Board of Governors. South Africa knew that the United States could not deliver this last demand in particular. It seemed determined to defy the United States and prevent international controls on its nuclear programme (Moore, 1987, p.115). Despite these developments the United States was not prepared to end its nuclear collaboration with South Africa on the grounds that it had to "retain a nuclear relationship in order to have influence to urge the South Africans to sign the Nonproliferation Treaty" (Lockwood, 1977, p.14). Andrew Young admitted that the United States was not about to end its long-standing policy of co-operation with South Africa in the development of its peaceful nuclear technology. He maintained that to cease nuclear co-operation at that stage would only encourage separate development of South Africa's own nuclear potential.[10] Eventually, it appeared that the American confrontation with South Africa served the latter's interests.

Deceleration

Thus, despite the Carter administration's initial euphoria and zeal, it became evident that things would not change as fast as expected. Mondale's interview in October 1977 with the *Rand Daily Mail*, a major South African newspaper, was some sort of a confession in this regard, where he stated that the United States wanted a good relationship with South Africa and that it had never proposed a plan in that country because Washington never had one. Mondale contradicted himself when he said that the central suggestion he had made in Vienna was that the leaders of the South African government meet with the legitimate non-White leaders of South Africa and develop with them reforms which were acceptable to all. He had by now realised, as had Kissinger before him, that "any official change would be dictated by the Afrikaner elites in the pursuit of their exclusive self-interests" (Jackson, 1982, pp.278-279). Commenting on American policy, Vorster said that it was fast reaching a stage where South Africa felt that the United States wanted to prescribe to them how they should run their country internally, which was unacceptable.[11] The American National Security Adviser Zbigniew Brzezinski, remarked that the United States was not asking for an instant change. It knew that this was a South African problem, but felt that unless there was domestic accommodation, international conflicts and tensions would grow.[12]

South Africa promptly provided new ammunition for its critics with the death of the Black Consciousness leader Steve Biko, in police custody on September 12, 1977; and the November crackdown on Black leadership. South African officials were dismayed when the American representative, Donald McHenry interrupted the negotiations over Namibia, to attend Biko's funeral.[13] The Carter administration led the international criticism following Biko's death and for a time it seemed as if it helped prevent death in detention in South Africa (Ungar and Vale, 1986, pp.263-264). The Congressional Black Caucus "resolution of concern" over the October bannings and arrests in South Africa, supported by Assistant Secretary Richard Moose was passed in the House of Representatives. On October 31, the United Nations Security Council adopted a resolution condemning apartheid in South Africa.[14]

The Arms Embargo

From 1963 to 1977 a United Nations voluntary arms embargo against South Africa was in existence. But the voluntary nature of the embargo was a direct loophole which defeated its very purpose. In November 1977 the United States joined the other members of the United Nations in voting for mandatory sanctions against arms transfers to South Africa.[15] The United States declared that it was supporting the embargo to reflect the international consensus that the supply of arms threatened peace. Secretary of State Cyrus Vance said that consistent with the embargo, the United States would prohibit all exports of items for the use of the police and military in South Africa. He went on to assure that there would be no more exports of spares and maintenance shipments for items whose export would be prohibited. In addition it was announced that the United States was withdrawing its naval attaché in Pretoria and recalling the commercial officer in Johannesburg, the latter being in connection with the review of American economic relations with South Africa (Vance, 1977b, pp.715-716).

However, when it came to economic sanctions against South Africa in the United Nations, the United States used its veto. Previously, at United Nations gatherings, both in Maputo and Lagos, Andrew Young had spoken against any form of substantive economic disengagement. The African resolutions for moderate economic sanctions had come just before the arms embargo. It was believed that the American support for the arms embargo was an ostensible attempt to exert pressure on South Africa without resorting to more drastic measures like trade and investment boycotts.[16] The administration was displaying an ambivalent policy of being morally outraged by apartheid on the one hand and deeply committed to finding substitutes for the use of force and economic sanctions on the other. As critics charged, the arms embargo was never totally effective and on several occasions some American corporations and their overseas affiliates were among those evading restrictions. Andrew Young perhaps summed up the likely effects of a mandatory embargo. He recognised the fact that South Africa had considerable self-sufficiency in arms and could get more or less what it wanted on the black market. In this sense, he said, a mandatory arms embargo was irrelevant although for psychological reasons it was found necessary.[17]

As early as August 1977, Julius Nyerere, President of Tanzania, commenting on the performance of the Carter administration had pointed out that the demand for human rights no longer appeared to be a stick with which to attack Communist states. He believed that it seemed to be a genuine effort to support justice in other states as well. All these, he thought, had given Africa renewed hope and the possibility of renewed faith in America (Nyerere, 1977b, p.45). On the other hand, critics maintained that the domestic priorities of the Carter administration so far did not reflect the demands of even those Blacks who had supported Carter. The veto of even the minimum economic disengagement and sanctions was contradictory to the advocacy of boycotts by South African Blacks. The administration was aware of this contradiction, but its spokesmen seemed to be indifferent and insensitive to the realities. It was a reminder to the South African

Blacks that the United States would never proceed beyond a certain limit. The administration's promise to embark on new directions in foreign policy amounted to nothing but rhetoric. Its position on human rights came to be dismissed as mere propaganda and any claim that it was guided by moral principles in the conduct of foreign policy was considered a matter of ridicule.

Enlightened Capitalism

It has been widely accepted that the Carter administration like its predecessors was reluctant to take steps that would harm American interests. From the beginning it had been faced with several major decisions on what attitude to take towards American investments as well as on bank loans to South Africa. The administration's attitude did not change from that of the previous administrations, that "the United States neither encourages nor discourages investment in South Africa". The ambivalence of that statement summed up the contradiction inherent in American policy towards South Africa. The refusal to take a position on the subject of American investment was considered to be a continuation of previous policies. In several circles it was argued that if appropriately planned, western investment could help raise living standards of Blacks and gradually force the political system to begin responding to Black aspirations. This position totally precluded any withdrawal of western capital on the grounds that the very people the West was supposedly concerned about helping, namely the South African Blacks would be affected by such a move. It was further argued that without western investment, the ongoing economic crisis in South Africa would be transferred into a major depression, depriving Black unskilled and semiskilled workers of their livelihood (Nagorski, 1978, pp.199-203).

It was the administration's belief that American economic presence in South Africa was a positive force. It placed great trust in the effectiveness of the Sullivan Principles. Reform, it maintained was more likely to result from internal socio-economic change, like the spread of the market, the growth of a Black middle class, Black consumerism and periodic non-violent boycotts. Young, on a visit to South Africa, upheld the supremacy of the free market system and reminded a group of mostly White South African business leaders that they had the key to change considered necessary to prevent the country's economic deterioration. He encouraged them to believe in their own power to overthrow apartheid. In Johannesburg, Young urged

Black South Africans to secure their rights through American style civil rights boycotts. Young's advocacy of capitalism was based on the belief that it was extremely fundamental, irreversible, pervasive and powerful that it amounted to a law of nature, the inevitability of which was also conveniently beneficial (Lockwood, 1977, p.12). These arguments, however, sounded unrealistic because the "market solution" could not begin to work effectively until after apartheid was formally dismantled. It looked like putting the cart before the horse. Unlike in the United States, in South Africa there were legal impediments to the growth of a substantial Black middle class (Goldsworthy, 1980, pp.232-233). Moreover such changes would take years or decades to become a reality.

American corporations were operating in South Africa on the basis of the "trickle down theory" which held that as foreign investments increased the national economy would prosper and the benefits would eventually "trickle down" to the general population. In a paper submitted to the Subcommittee on International Economic Policy and Trade and the Subcommittee on Africa, of the House Committee on Foreign Affairs, Elizabeth Schmidt stated that history had exposed the weakness of the corporate argument. The theory had not worked. While the South African Gross Domestic Product had increased by more than 2000 per cent since the end of World War II, very little of that increase had benefited South Africa's Black majority. Most of the Blacks continued to subsist below the poverty line. As in the case of economic growth, the projected increase in social and political rights had failed to materialise. In reality, economic abundance had been accompanied by an intensification of political repression (*United States Policy Toward South Africa*, 1980, pp.800-806). One statement before the House Committee on Foreign Affairs highlighted the thesis that corporations could more vigorously implement change than the past record showed. It pointed out that the penalty for failure had to be disinvestment. Those who favoured the peaceful demise of apartheid often appealed to prudence. "Prudence is meaningless in South Africa. It stifles creative undermining of apartheid", it said (*United States Policy Toward South Africa*, 1980, pp.896-905).

The administration was reluctant to commit real political or economic power to secure the changes in South Africa which it claimed to seek. Many considered the administration to have taken up a pragmatic version of Tar Baby. South Africa, with its strength and stability was found to be the prime guarantor of profits for American entrepreneurs. American firms with a stake in South Africa influenced the administration for their benefit. The maximum they proceeded with regard to South Africa was adherence to the Sullivan Principles. Punitive measures were opposed because they would harm their economic interests. A number of measures directed at restricting foreign investment in South Africa were introduced in the United States Congress in 1978. But none of these bills were approved. Even representatives of the Departments of State, Treasury and Commerce argued against legislative restrictions on the ground that they would limit the administration's flexibility to respond to the situation in South Africa.[18] Carter advocated capitalism and non-violence rather than sanctions, and the use of carrots instead of sticks to pursue a Southern Africa policy.

The Nigerian Factor

The Nigerian factor in American policy towards South Africa came to the fore in 1978. Nigeria had begun to spearhead a major antiapartheid movement and assumed the role of an important economic power in Africa. Nigeria was also supplying the United States with a sizeable amount of oil, and the volume of United States-Nigeria trade had become something like double the volume of American trade with South Africa. At the same time Nigeria impressed upon the United States that it was not interested in improved bilateral relations as long as the latter continued its support for the status quo in Southern Africa (Bach, 1983, pp.33-55; Herkovits, 1977-1978, pp.167-168). In view of its dependence on Nigerian oil, the United States could no longer remain insensitive to the latter's pressure on Namibian decolonisation and its militancy on Southern African affairs. To acknowledge Nigeria's importance, Carter paid a visit to that country in April 1978, where he declared that Nigeria was among the leaders of international efforts to bring the principles of majority rule and individual rights into reality in Southern Africa. He also expressed the hope that South African society would be transformed progressively and peacefully (Carter, 1979a, pp.309-310).

But the American collaboration with Nigeria, while raising expectations of the Black people in Southern Africa only made the South African regime recalcitrant. South African Whites came to regard Carter as their greatest enemy because he was trying to humiliate or destroy them. Vorster attacked Carter's policies in Africa and the human rights campaign as expressions of selective morality if there were any moral principles involved.[19] South Africa ultimately withdrew from its role of co-operating with the United States to secure the end of White rule in Rhodesia.

Divergent Approaches

Within the administration, on the question of South Africa, the conflict was between two approaches. On the one hand was communication and persuasion, and on the other was pressure and isolation. Advocates of the first approach maintained that through closer ties, particularly economic, the United States could help the Whites find a way to liberalise South African society. The defenders of the second approach rejected this view on the ground that three decades of economic growth had not produced fundamental change and that foreign investment had only helped strengthen the repressive system. The primary charge levelled against the second approach was that by cutting off economic and other ties with South Africa, change could not be forced, because South Africa could survive such pressures. Moreover, it would drive South Africa into isolation and damage American economic interests.

Carter and Vance reaffirmed the need for affirmative policies. Vance (1979a, p.334) stated that the United States had no wish to see South African Whites driven out of the home of their ancestors but hoped that they would live in peace and justice with their fellow citizens. In his noted Annapolis speech, Carter stated that the United States wanted to see an Africa that was free from the dominance of outside powers, of racial injustice, of conflict and the burden of poverty, hunger and disease. He also stated that they were convinced that the best way to work towards these objectives was through affirmative policies that recognised African realities and aspirations (Carter, 1979b, p.209).

Realpolitik Attempts a Comeback

The second half of Carter's presidency saw a mellowing of the enthusiasm of fostering change in South Africa. Even in the case of the overall American policy towards sub Saharan Africa, the administration was losing interest in involvement. Congressional elections in the United States in 1978 had strengthened the conservatives both in the Republican and Democratic Parties. By now the United States had accepted the fact that South African co-operation was necessary for a Namibian settlement. Carter's rhetoric on South African issues subsided. This was attributed to the fact that the practitioners of realpolitik had gained the upper hand in the administration. Those who were expecting economic sanctions against South Africa were disappointed. It was not clear whether any of the administration's previous policies and strategies vis à vis South Africa remained operative. Vance (1979b, pp.42-43) admitted to a group of Afro-American leaders that change in South Africa was a long and difficult process, and that the United States had put forward neither a blueprint nor a timetable for change, which was for the people of South Africa to decide together. Dick Clark, addressing the African-American Conference in Khartoum, said that the United States was at "a crossroads of decision" with regard to its policy towards Africa. It had to decide whether to step back into anti-Communist preoccupations or advance into new frontiers (Clark, 1979, p.14).

The hanging of Black nationalist Solomon Mahalangu and the expulsion of American military attachés from South Africa were two incidents in 1979 which were irritants in American-South African relations. President Carter's plea for clemency for Mahalangu was not heeded by the South African government. Shortly after this, in April 1979, three military attachés serving at the United States Embassy in Pretoria were expelled for taking photographs of the Valindaba plant from the American ambassador's plane. In retaliation, the United States expelled all but one of the South African military attachés from Washington. In May 1979 South Africa attempted to take its seat at the United Nations General Assembly when the question of Namibia was being discussed. The move was resisted by the majority. Andrew Young criticised this decision and said that the forum was also meant for the purpose of listening to those with whom one disagreed and those representatives, though not selected by the free and independent choice of all its citizens, represented the governments of those states.[20] These were the very governments that Young had once described "illegitimate".

There was further decline in American activism on South Africa with the resignation of Andrew Young as the Ambassador to the United Nations.[21] One hurdle in the way of an activist foreign policy was the backlash of the White minority government against American pressure. Another was the congressional attitude in favour of lifting sanctions against Rhodesia, which made the prospect of pressure against South Africa increasingly unlikely (Ottaway, 1979, pp.639-640).

During Carter's last year in office, events in Iran and Afghanistan distracted attention from South Africa. In Southern Africa itself all attention was on Rhodesia. Being election year in the United States, for many in the administration it was a year of stock taking rather than initiative on South Africa. Assistant Secretary Moose's statements were a far cry from the ones issued four years back. He pointed out that the United States had interests in preserving national consensus on foreign policy goals relating to human rights, assuring long term access to strategic minerals, and foreclosing opportunities for expanded Soviet influence. These interests, he maintained, could not be pursued selectively. Without political change, American humanitarian interests could not be fulfilled, the risk of violent conflict was growing and the possibilities for Soviet meddling were increasing (Moose, 1980, p.20). Regarding American policy towards South Africa, Moose stated that there was no retreat from the commitment to change. The main thrust of American policy was to encourage peaceful but rapid change. The United States, he said, accepted the fact that it had limited influence. But it would work with other western countries in encouraging South Africa to avoid the tragedy of self-destruction (*United States Policy Toward South Africa*, 1980, pp.4-7). Andrew Young, writing in *Foreign Affairs*, pointed out that only the Soviet invasion of Afghanistan and an anti-draft protest had undercut the South African issue in 1980. Referring to the strong moral case for divestiture that was gaining ground, he admitted that corporate America had to eventually choose between a market of four million White South Africans and a market of four hundred million Blacks of the entire continent of Africa. He warned against a return to the period four years back when American influence was at its lowest in Africa. Young stressed the need for the United States to foster conflict resolution. He however, wanted the United States to capitalise on the "mutual interests in a profitable economic relationship" with Africa (Young, 1980, pp.648-666).

The Two Front Attack

Criticism of Carter's South Africa policy came from both Republicans and Democrats. Chester Crocker, who was later to become Ronald Reagan's Assistant Secretary of State for African Affairs was one of the antagonists of the policy. In an article written for *Foreign Affairs* in 1980, he argued that the Carter administration had tilted too far towards Black Africa with little to show for it. He maintained that reform in South Africa and a settlement in Namibia were unlikely to be achieved by further alienating the

South African government. The Carter policy was described as an ambitious regional policy, one which saw an identity of American and African interests and affirmed that the very existence of the West's private sector could serve as a surrogate for a coherent strategy. Crocker was critical of both the globalists and regionalists in the administration for misreading the African reality (Crocker, 1980-1981, pp.323-351; Crocker, 1980, p.82). At the Congressional hearings in 1980, he stated that it was politically in the interests of the United States that there be a steady and relatively orderly movement towards a non-racial South Africa with which it was possible to pursue a full and normal relationship. Such a change was to be favoured because it was consistent with American principles and the commitment to human rights and the only way to avoid a major human tragedy in South Africa. Other American interests, he said, would inevitably suffer if such change failed to occur (*United States Policy Toward South Africa*, 1980, p.375).

The Carter policy was launched with great pressure on South Africa to accede to majority rule. The initial expectation was that a victorious coalition of White liberals and non-White dissidents would emerge, powerful enough to force the government into submission. But the White regime responded with force. The Carter administration's support to antiapartheid groups was restricted only to verbal support and there was no commitment beyond this. An observer stated in 1980 that the United States had negligible influence at that moment with the South African government and would almost certainly have failed in any effort to establish a productive ongoing bilateral relationship, the intention of which was to secure continued constructive change. He maintained that despite this corporations, banks, private organisations and even academics could make substantial contributions to strengthen the prospects for policy change. Another observer held that the United States had too often acted in ways that supported the apartheid status quo. He stated that restrictions on new investments and future bank loans were the least the United States could do to show its seriousness in supporting full human rights for all in South Africa (*United States Policy Toward South Africa*, 1980, pp.56, 602-605).

The Carter administration was perhaps not as much concerned about the Cold War as its Republican predecessors, but it was not entirely indifferent to its existence. While the administration constantly insisted that it was interested in the problems of underdevelopment rather than the rivalry with the Soviet Union, in the words of Eidelburg (1981, p.65) this was a "specious distinction". The United States was concerned with the increasing diplomatic and economic clout of Third World countries like Nigeria because their support was needed to prosecute the Cold War. Young and McHenry were just as anti-Soviet and just as committed to the objectives of international capitalism and the pursuance of American realpolitik as their predecessors. Where they differed was mostly in the issue of style, the Carter administration's tone being more vociferous and self-righteous. Some critics went one step ahead in criticising Young. They described him as the final compromise between Black petty bourgeoisie and the White ruling class. They felt that the pseudo-liberals of the White ruling class used people like Young to take advantage of the international sympathy for Afro-Americans and promote the Afro-American success image in order to entice Africa and the Third World into a trap of highly controlled imperialism (Newsum and Abengunrin, 1987).

Despite its good intentions and head start on Southern Africa, by the end of 1980, the Carter policy was facing difficulties. The policy was not able to withstand the toughest tests and was inconclusive at other times. In Congress there was substantial opposition to greater involvement in Africa. The supporters of greater involvement in Africa lost their spokesmen when Dick Clark failed to get himself re-elected and Charles Diggs had to give up his committee chairmanship for other reasons. In the final stages of the administration, there was a general confusion about human rights as an issue in international politics and the manner in which such issues could be handled. The Carter administration had initially launched a policy which rejected Kissinger's globalist approach to Africa's problems for a regional approach. Towards the end it looked as if it was making a reversal to the Kissingerian view. Nolutshungu (1985, p.58) in his brief summary of the administration's policy states that, "while it would serve no purpose to speculate whether Carter's policy would ever have any success in changing South Africa itself, it is clear that from the start his policy was never as radical as it sounded".

In 1980, the election year, Carter's greatest challenge and criticism regarding his South Africa policy came from the Republican platform. It highlighted the Soviet gains in Southern Africa resulting from Carter's policy. Senator Robert Dole, a leading contender for the Republican ticket blamed the administration for alienating the South African leadership and expressed the fear that the Soviet Union appeared to have selected Africa as a "staging ground for a strategic showdown, to test the will of the United States" (Deutsch, 1979a, p.56).

The Carter administration had given much hope to those who believed that the United States could use its power and influence to secure change in South Africa. But it could not fulfil its promises. Eventually the administration faced harsh criticism not only from its opponents but also from its supporters. The latter were disillusioned at being let down by an administration in which they had placed much faith. The intentions of the administration were good, but in the absence of broad commitments and actions, nothing could be accomplished.

Notes

1. *The Sunday Times* (London), May 15, 1977.
2. Vice President Mondale's statement, Vienna, May 20, 1977, Document 618, *American Foreign Policy Basic Documents, 1977-1980* (1983), Department of State, Washington, DC.
3. *The Statesman* (New Delhi) May 23, 1977.
4. *International Herald Tribune* (Paris), June 10, 1977.
5. *International Herald Tribune* (Paris), June 23, 1977.
6. *International Herald Tribune* (Paris), May 7, 1977.
7. At the time when Vance made his speech, there was a policy disagreement within the Department of State. Vance's human rights approach was opposed by National Security Adviser Brzezinski who advocated a Cold War stance in relation to Southern African issues.
8. *Transnational Corporations, Activities of Transnational Corporations in Southern Africa: Impact on Financial and Social Structure* (1978), United Nations, New York, pp. 14-16.
9. "The Sullivan Principles: No Cure for Apartheid, A Public Statement", Statement before the Subcommittee on International Economic Policy and Trade; and the Subcommittee on Africa; House Committee on Foreign Affairs, May 15, 1980, *United States Policy Toward South Africa* (1980), 96th Congress, Second Session, Government Printing Office, Washington , DC, p. 347.
10. *International Herald Tribune* (Paris), November 2, 1977.
11. *International Herald Tribune* (Paris), September 19, 1977.
12. Zbigniew Brzezinski, National Security Adviser, replies to questions asked on CBS "Face the Nation". October 30, 1977, Document 624, *American Foreign Policy Basic Documents, 1977-1980* (1983), Department of State, Washington, DC.
13. McHenry was leading the five Western nation "Contact Group" to negotiate terms for Namibia's independence on the basis of free nationwide elections under United Nations supervision.
14. *General Assembly Official Records*, Resolution 417 (XXXII), October 31, 1977.
15. *General Assembly Official Records*, Resolution 418 (XXXII), November 4, 1977.
16. *The Times* (London), October 29, 1977.
17. *Economic Times* (New Delhi), November 8, 1977.

18. *The Activities of Transnational Corporations in the Industrial, Mining and Military Sectors of Southern Africa* (1980), United Nations Centre on Transnational Corporations, New York, p. 9.
19. *International Herald Tribune* (Paris), April 23, 1978.
20. Statement by Andrew Young before the United Nations General Assembly, May 24, 1979, Document 629, *America's Foreign Policy Basic Documents, 1977-1980* (1983), Department of State, Washington, DC.
21. Young had to resign over a controversy surrounding his meeting with a representative of the Palestine Liberation Organisation.

7 Conclusion

Apartheid in South Africa was an issue which plagued United States foreign policy for several years. Through the years the United States has persistently emphasised the significance of its ideals for all humanity. More than any other nation it has constantly reiterated that its institutions and policies have reflected these ideals and that the American mission was directed at their promotion externally for the benefit of all humanity, particularly the oppressed peoples of the world.

In the sphere of foreign policy, one of the most severe challenges for the United States came from South Africa. The very nature of apartheid based on inequality and servitude made it totally irreconcilable and antithetical to American morals, values and sensibilities. The analysis made in the preceding pages makes it clear that the United States failed to uphold its self proclaimed ideals in the case of its relations with South Africa. American disapproval of apartheid could have been expressed through measures like non-recognition, dissociation and the imposition of economic sanctions. But over the years it resorted only to verbal interventionism and half-measures which proved ineffective in influencing South Africa to reform its inhuman racist system. Even the half-measures it took were only intended to maintain its standing at the international level particularly within the Third World, while at the same time safeguarding its interests. In essence, American policies contradicted the professed belief of the United States in ideals like equality, liberty and democracy, thus questioning its claim to be the champion of freedom.

The economic and strategic interests of the United States in South Africa played a crucial role in shaping American policy. Although American trade and investment in South Africa was between 1 per cent and 2 per cent of the former's global total, in monetary terms these figures were not insignificant amounting as they did to millions of dollars. Moreover, South Africa was the United States best customer in Africa. South Africa's mineral resources have always been important to the United States. Although the United States often had enough supplies for existing levels of production, the enormous and unprecedented growth and achievement of high levels of production increased the demand for minerals which could not be met from internal sources alone. And when it came to certain minerals like chromium, United States domestic reserves were not sufficient and consequently it had to rely more on South African supplies. Moreover, for some of the minerals, the alternative supplier happened to be the Soviet Union. South Africa's geographic location and strategic importance was another factor in the making of American policy. The growing importance of the Indian Ocean in the nineteen seventies raised South Africa's status in American strategic thinking. The Cape sea route is one of the busiest sea lanes in the world and is also the main passage for the oil tankers of the West particularly the United States. The Arab-Israeli war and the oil crisis of 1973 had clearly demonstrated the importance of the Cape route in comparison with the Suez route. Cold War considerations and the American conflict with the Soviet Union enhanced the position of South Africa. The White minority regime in South Africa was strongly anti-Communist, was keen on the maintenance of the status quo and was prepared to act as a regional surrogate for the United States. In this context it has to be noted that the argument that stringent American action against South Africa would lead it to the Soviet camp was baseless.

Viewing the issue from the South African perspective, relations with the United States contributed to its economic well-being and security. American trade and investment formed a significant portion of its economy. Furthermore, the United States was the best customer for its minerals. The strategic ties with the United States strengthened its position in Southern Africa, thus protecting it to a great extent from its hostile neighbours and liberation movements, some of which with Communist assistance were seeking to overthrow the minority regime. Above all, United States diplomatic support at international forums, including its use of the veto at the United Nations made it an indispensable ally. The relationship was one of reciprocity, one in which there were various common interests.

Consequently, more than any other country in the world, the United States had some influence on South Africa, one which many Americans were reluctant to admit. But American concerns were not over the violations of ideals in South Africa or the situation of the Blacks there but rather with safeguarding its material interests. Regarding the rationale and desirability of the United States associating only with regimes that adhere to American ideals, it may be argued that most governments have violated them in one way or the other and that a foreign policy based on this criterion would bring it many enemies and few friends. But here lies the danger of equating South Africa with other countries which have violated these ideals. The South

African case was without parallel. The very character of the system of apartheid defies any attempt to equate it with other oppressive systems, for in South Africa racial discrimination was legally enshrined.

An examination of the three American administrations reveals that their approaches differed only in style, not substance. The outcome of their policies amounted to the same and there was no effect on South Africa or on change in the overall situation in that country.

The Nixon administration's priorities did not include South Africa. Consequently, adequate attention was not paid to the issues regarding that country. The National Security Study Memorandum 39 (NSSM 39) spread a false impression that the administration was paying increased attention to Southern Africa. But it was only one among the many such reviews world-wide and was meant to reorganise American policy and tide over the differences within the administration over South Africa. The adoption of Option Two of NSSM 39 was to prove unrealistic and revealed the short-sightedness of American policy. The administration's concern was with Communism, not racism. The American perceptions of the Cold War coloured its policy towards South Africa. The administration assumed that White minority regimes would remain in power for a considerable period and that constructive change would come only through them. It also believed that the Blacks in Southern Africa would not receive their political rights through violence but only as a concession from White regimes. At the same time the administration did not want to give the impression that it was supporting apartheid. Statements emanating from the administration indicated that the United States was committed to American ideals and that the dedication to them was a result of its history and a product of its search for the basic answers to human aspirations.

The Nixon administration maintained that it was most important to keep open the lines of communication so that it could use its influence constructively to persuade South Africa to reform. It diluted the existing arms embargo and began co-operating with South Africa in different spheres. Its attitude at the United Nations was only helpful to South Africa. It took a pro-South African stand on issues regarding the Air Transport Agreement and the Sugar Quota issue and refused to regard apartheid a crime against humanity. The Nixon administration failed to comprehend the danger of the explosive situation in South Africa and was concerned only with the maintenance of the status quo. It felt that if change was to occur at all, it had to be slow and evolutionary. Rewards instead of punishments were used to influence South Africa. Although international opinion was critical of such moves, the administration preferred to disregard it for the sake of its communication policy and its interests in South Africa. In short, the policy showed a cynical lack of concern which was in sharp contrast to the public platitudes and pronouncements of its spokesmen.

The Ford administration was to a great extent a victim of the Southern Africa policy of its predecessor. It had to face the realities arising out of a situation where the assumptions based on Option Two of NSSM 39 were shattered, and realised the need for a new approach. The administration, however, saw no reason to tamper with South African apartheid because the White minority regime in that country protected American interests and appeared relatively stable. The purpose of a new approach, in the form of the Kissinger initiative, was to ensure the security of South Africa where the United States had considerable interests which were to be protected even at the cost of Namibia and the White minority regime of Rhodesia. Armed struggle had to be circumvented to prevent the chances of intervention by outside powers including the Soviet Union.

Promoting controlled change in Southern Africa thus became the objective of the Ford administration. The new policy was described by itself as one of humanitarian concern for peaceful change. In an unprecedented move the administration confessed its neglect of the region in the past because of its responsibilities elsewhere in the world. It began making efforts to influence South Africa in order to persuade Rhodesia to accede to majority rule. To South Africa, the United States signalled that it would give it time to enact a mild programme of economic and social reform, in exchange for co-operation on Rhodesia. Nothing was mentioned about political reform. It was stated that American policy towards South Africa was based on the premise that within a reasonable time there would be a clear evolution towards equality of opportunity and basic human rights for all South Africans. The policy was regarded with scepticism by many observers as it was concerned only about White minority rule in Rhodesia but not in South Africa. This cynicism appeared reasonable considering South Africa's credentials to persuade Rhodesia to accede to majority rule. The Ford administration had no programme to bring change in South Africa. Its strategy was to align more closely with the apartheid regime to secure settlements in Rhodesia and Namibia and also to buy time for the South African government to reform its own system. Eventually the administration could not bring about any concrete settlement in Rhodesia and was subject to criticism of its policy by those who were unconvinced of its new-found humanitarian approach.

When the Carter administration assumed office, it was widely believed that its policies would differ drastically from those of its predecessors. Carter seemed to place great emphasis on moral values and human rights which were an essential part of American ideals. The administration wanted to dissociate its behaviour in Africa from American competitiveness with the Soviet Union. It realised that the credibility of the United States would be enhanced particularly among the Black African states only if they believed that it was not committed to perpetuating White supremacy in Southern Africa. The American bona fides therefore lay in its ability to apply pressure on South Africa to dismantle apartheid. The administration arrived at the conclusion that Southern African problems were to be regarded as urgent, that the United States should remain committed to peaceful solutions, since guerrilla warfare could be exploited by the Soviet Union in its own interests and that the United States had to co-operate with others in finding solutions. With regard to South Africa it stressed the need for the United States to take a stronger stand against apartheid, or imperil its relations with the Third World. The administration made it clear to South Africa that change had to occur there without waiting for settlements elsewhere. Above all, the administration proclaimed that its human rights policies as far as South Africa was concerned had to reflect American ideals. The Carter administration wanted to distance itself from South Africa and convince the world that it was serious about its tougher policy towards that country. It gave strong support to the Sullivan Principles and created a furore over South Africa's nuclear programme. It joined the United Nations in voting for a mandatory arms embargo against South Africa and condemned government repression and judicial murders there. The sale of equipment which could be used for military purposes was prohibited and several personnel from its mission in South Africa were recalled. Furthermore, it unleashed a verbal tirade against South Africa.

Despite the Carter administration's initial euphoria, it soon realised that changes in South Africa would not occur as fast as anticipated. South Africa was not responding in a manner that the administration expected. The former began giving the impression that it could withstand any kind of external pressure. Furthermore, the United States felt that South African support was essential in order to reach settlements on Rhodesia and Namibia. It therefore felt the need to co-operate with South Africa at the diplomatic level. The Sullivan Principles evoked limited response. At the United Nations the administration vetoed economic sanctions against South Africa and refused any kind of economic disengagement with it. It believed that American capitalism could play a positive role through its operations in South Africa. Reform, it maintained, was to occur as a result of socio-economic change like the spread of the market, growth of a Black middle class, Black consumerism and by periodic non-violent boycotts. In other words, it advocated an American style civil rights movement for South Africa. In essence, it took only those steps which would not harm American economic interests, claiming that economic measures would only harm the Black majority in South Africa. Towards the second half of its term, the Carter administration lost its zeal for involvement in the affairs of South Africa. Moreover, within the administration, the practitioners of realpolitik gained an upper hand. Members of the administration admitted that change in South Africa was a long and difficult process, that the United States had no blueprint for change and that it was for the people of South Africa themselves to draw a timetable for change. The Carter administration realised the failure of its human rights approach as well as that of enlightened capitalism. Ultimately it alienated South Africa. The administration simultaneously disappointed its adherents who had expected far reaching changes both in American policy and the South African system.

Thus, an analysis of the policies of the aforesaid period makes it evident that United States administrations had not been successful in upholding American ideals in the context of South Africa. These ideals are considered to be the cornerstone of American foreign policy. Although it had the capability to utilise its leverage with South Africa, it failed miserably through the lack of realistic policies. Non-intervention on behalf of the oppressed in South Africa in effect meant intervention on the side of the White minority regime. The American attitude lacked foresight despite the fact that it was a generally accepted conclusion that in the long run the struggle against apartheid would prevail and that a Black majority government would come to power in South Africa. It was evident that in such circumstances the United States would have to reckon with the new realities and pay the price for its past policies. American policymakers opted for short term solutions for problems with long term implications. Inaction coupled with rhetoric thus questioned the very rationale of United States policy towards South Africa.

One of the arguments put forth in this book at the outset itself was that the United States did not utilise the opportunity to use its economic power in the form of sanctions against South Africa. Some observers were sceptical because they thought that punitive economic sanctions would be effective only as threats and would be withstood by the White minority.

They also argued that the Blacks would ultimately suffer because of sanctions. Until 1986 administrations in the United States could insulate themselves from the demands for economic sanctions. By then, antiapartheid organisations within the United States were able to mobilise public opinion so much so that Congress eventually enacted economic sanctions against South Africa. Succeeding events in South Africa proved that sanctions worked. When American banks refused to help South Africa over its debt problems, an economic crisis was precipitated in the country. Capital flowed out of South Africa, inflation increased and the annual growth rate went down. Sanctions ultimately had an effect on White South African thinking. With the collapse of the Soviet Union and the developments in East Europe, the much projected threat from them no longer existed, thus questioning the rationale for continued American ties with the White minority government of South Africa.

It would also be difficult to ignore the fact that more than American adherence to its ideals, hard facts forced the United States to impose sanctions. The burgeoning crisis in South Africa and the minority regime's acknowledgement that apartheid was becoming outdated and unacceptable indicated the inevitability of the collapse of apartheid. For the United States the message was clear–only substantial change in policy would guarantee its stakes in a post apartheid South Africa.

In essence it may be stated that it was not ideals which guided United States policy towards South Africa but rather its economic and strategic interests. Although apartheid was in total contradiction to American ideals, the United States pursued a policy that was devoid of humanitarian values and one which abandoned the oppressed people of South Africa to the inhuman system of apartheid.

Bibliography

Allison, Roy and Williams, Phil. (1990), *Superpower Competition and Crisis Prevention in the Third World*, Cambridge University Press, Cambridge.

Ayoob, Mohammad (ed) (1980), *Conflict and Intervention in the Third World*, Croom Helm, London.

Bach, Daniel C. (1983), "Nigerian-American Relations: Converging Interests and Power Relations" in Timothy M. Shaw and Olajide Aluko (eds), *Nigerian Foreign Policy: Alternative Perceptions and Projections*, Macmillan, London.

Bailey, Thomas A. (1990). *A Diplomatic History of the American People*, Prentice Hall, New Delhi.

Baker, James E., de St Jorre, John and O'Flaherty, J. Daniel (1979), "The American Consensus on South Africa", *Worldview* (New York), vol. 22(10), pp.12-16.

Ball, George W. (1976), "The Disenchantment With Kissinger", *Saturday Review* (New York), (June 12), pp.20-22.

--- (1977), "Asking for Trouble in South Africa", *The Atlantic Monthly* (Boston), (October), pp.43-51.

Barber, James (1973), *South Africa's Foreign Policy: 1945-1970*, Oxford University Press, London.

Bender, Gerald J., Coleman, James S. and Sklar, Richard L. (eds) (1985), *African Crisis Areas and US Foreign Policy*, University of California Press, Berkeley and Los Angeles.

Berridge, Geoff R. (1990), "The Superpowers and Southern Africa", in Roy Allison and Phil Williams (eds), *Superpower Competiton and Crisis Prevention in the Third World*, Cambridge University Press, Cambridge.

Bertolin, Gordon (1978), "US Economic Interests in Africa: Investment Trade and Raw Materials", in Jennifer Seymour Whitaker (ed), *Africa and United States: Vital Interests*, New York University Press, New York.

Bissel, Richard E. (1977), "United States Policy in Africa", *Current History* (Philadelphia), vol.73 (432).

--- (1982), *South Africa and the United States: The Erosion of an Influence Relationship*, Praeger, New York.

Blashill, John (1972), "The Proper Role of US Corporations in South Africa", *Fortune* (New York), (July), pp.49-53, 89-91.

Boateng, E. A. (1978), *A Political Geography of Africa*, Cambridge University Press, Cambridge.

Bowman, Larry (1982), "The Strategic Importance of South Africa to the United States: An Appraisal and Policy Analysis", *African Affairs* (Oxford), vol.81(323), pp.159-191.

--- and Clark, Ian (eds) (1983), *The Indian Ocean in Global Politics*, Young India, New Delhi.

Browett, John (1982), "The Evolution of Unequal Development Within South Africa: An Overview", in David M. Smith (ed), *Living Under Apartheid*, George Allen and Unwin, London.

Bunting, Brian (1969), *The Rise of the South African Reich*, Penguin, Harmondsworth.

Burner, David (1988), *John F. Kennedy and a New Generation*, Scott, Foresman and Co., Glenview, Illinois.

Burns, James MacGregor (1990), *The Crosswinds of Freedom*, Asian Books, New Delhi.

Callaghy, Thomas M. (ed) (1983), *South Africa in Southern Africa: The Intensifying Vortex of Violence*, Praeger, New York.

Callinicos, Alex and Rogers, John (1977), *Southern Africa After Soweto*, Pluto Press, London.

Canham, Erwin D. (1964), *The Ethics of United States Foreign Relations, The Paul Anthony Brick Lectures*, University of Missouri Press, Columbia.

Carter, Jimmy (1977a), *A Government as Good as Its People*, Simon and Schuster, New York.

--- (1977b), *Public Papers of Presidents, 1977*, Government Printing Office, Washington, DC.

--- (1979a), "Reaffirming US Policy", in Elaine P. Adam (ed), *American Foreign Relations, 1978: A Documentary Record*, New York University Press, New York.

--- (1979b), "The United States and the Soviet Union", in Elaine P. Adam (ed), *American Foreign Relations, 1978: A Documentary Record*, New York University Press, New York.

Clark, Dick (1977), "American Policy Toward Southern Africa Under a New Administration", *Issue* (Waltham), vol.7(1), pp.1-4.

--- (1979), "US-African Policy at the Crossroads", *Africa Report* (New York), vol.24(1), pp.12-14.

Clement, Peter (1985), "Moscow and Southern Africa", *Problems of Communism* (Washington, DC), vol.34(2), pp.29-50.

Coker, Christopher (1986), *The United States and South Africa, 1968-1985: Constructive Engagement and Its Critics*, Duke University Press, Durham.

Crabb, Cecil V. (1976), *Policy-Makers and Critics: Conflicting Theories of American Foreign Policy*, Praeger, New York.

Crocker, Chester A. (1980), "African Policy in the 1980s", *The Washington Quarterly* (Cambridge, MA), vol. 8(3), pp.72-86.

--- (1980-1981), "South Africa: Strategy for Change", *Foreign Affairs* (New York), vol.59(2), pp.323-351.

Curtis, Neville (1972), "South Africa: The Politics of Fragmentation", *Foreign Affairs* (New York), vol.50(2), pp.283-296.

Darnston, John (1976), "Kissinger's African Mission: The Intricacies", *Dawn* (Karachi), (September 22).

Davenport, T.R.H. (1987), *South Africa: A Modern History*, Macmillan, Basingstoke.

Davidson, Appolon (1984), *Cecil Rhodes and His Time*, Progress Publishers, Moscow.

Davis, Jennifer (1977), "US Dollars in South Africa: Context and Consequence", *Issue* (Waltham), vol.7(4), pp.17-22.

Deutsch, Richard (1979a), "The Republican Challenge on Africa", *Africa Report* (New York), vol.24(3), pp.55-57.

--- (1979b), "African Oil and US Foreign Policy", *Africa Report* (New York), vol.24(5), pp.47-51.

Diggs, Charles (1971), *Congresssional Record*, June 3.

Dow, John (1971), *Congressional Record*, April 1.

Dowdy, William L. and Trood, Russell B. (eds) (1985), *The Indian Ocean: Perspectives on a Strategic Arena*, Duke University Press, Durham.

Du Jonchay, Yvan (1978), *The Handbook of World Transport*, Macmillan, London.

Dugard, John (1978), *Human Rights and the South African Legal Order*, Princeton University Press, Princeton, NJ.

Duignan, Peter and Gann, L. H. (1984), *The United States and Africa: A History*, Cambridge University Press, Cambridge.

--- and Rabushka, Alvin (eds) (1980), *The United States in the 1980s*, Croom Helm and Hoover Institution Press, Stanford.

Duncan, Patrick (1963), "Towards a World Policy for South Africa", *Foreign Affairs* (New York), vol.42(1), pp.38-48.

Eidelburg, P. G. (1981), "US-RSA Relations: A Rejoinder–Back to the Halls of Montezuma?", *Africa Insight* (Pretoria), vol.11(2), pp.60-67.

Ekirch, Arthur A. (1966), *Ideas, Ideals and American Diplomacy: A History of their Growth and Interaction*, Appleton-Century-Crofts, New York.

El Khawas, Mohammed A. and Cohen, Barry (eds) (1976), National Security Study Memorandum 39: The Kissinger Study of Southern Africa, Lawrence Hill, Westport, Connecticut.

Ferrel, Robert H. (1975), *American Diplomacy: A History*, Norton, New York.

Fine, Daniel I. (1977), "Africa After Kissinger", *Worldview* (New York), vol.20(4), pp.22-23.

Foltz, William J. (1985), "United States Policy Toward South Africa: Is One Possible?", in Gerald J. Bender, James S. Coleman and Richard L. Sklar (eds), *African Crisis Areas and US Foreign Policy*, University of California Press, Berkeley and Los Angeles.

--- (1986), "United States Military and Strategic Interests in Africa" in Elliot P. Skinner (ed), *Beyond Constructive Engagement: United States Foreign Policy Toward Africa*, Paragon House, New York.

Ford, Gerald (1974), "President Ford Pledges Continuity in Foreign Policy", *Department of State Bulletin*, vol.71 (1836).

--- (1976), "President Ford Pledges US Support for Solution in Southern Africa", *Department of State Bulletin*, vol.75 (1948).

Foreign Policy Implications of Racial Exclusion in Granting Visas (1970), House Committee on Foreign Affairs, 91st Congress, Second Session, Government Printing Office, Washington, DC.

Frank, Thomas M. and Weisband, Edward (1979), *Foreign Policy by Congress*, Oxford University Press, New York.

Frankel, Charles (1975), *Morality and US Foreign Policy*, Foreign Policy Association, New York.

Gann, L. H. and Duignan, Peter (1980), "Africa", in Peter Duignan and Alvin Rabushka (eds), *The United States in the 1980s*, Croom Helm and Hoover Institution Press, Stanford.

--- --- (1981), *Why South Africa will Survive: A Historical Analysis*, Croom Helm, London.

Geldenhuys, Deon (1984), *The Diplomacy of Isolation: South African Policy Making*, Macmillan South Africa, Johannesburg.

Golan, Galia (1988), *The Soviet Union and National Liberation Movements in the Third World*, Unwin Hyman, Boston.

Goldberg, Arthur (1968), "Statement to the United Nations", *Department of State Bulletin*, vol.58 (1490).

Goldsworthy, D. J. (1980), "South Africa" in Mohammed Ayoob (ed), *Conflict and Intervention in the Third World*, Croom Helm, London.

Graebner, Norman A. (1978), *The Age of Global Power: The United States Since 1939*, John Wiley, New York.

— (1984), *America as a World Power*, Scholarly Resources Inc., Wilmington.

Graham, Hugh Davis (1990), *The Civil Rights Era: Origins and Development of National Policy*, Oxford University Press, New York.

Grundy, Kenneth W. (1986), *The Militarization of South African Politics*, I. B. Tauris, London.

Gunther, John (1955), *Inside Africa*, Harper and Row, New York.

Haines, Gerald K. and Walker, J. Samuel (eds) (1981), *American Foreign Relations: A Historiographical Review*, Frances Pinter, London.

Hanks, Robert J. (1983), *Southern Africa and Western Security*, Institute for Foreign Policy Analysis, Cambridge, MA.

Hartz, Louis (1955), *The Liberal Tradition in America*, Harcourt, Brace and World, Inc., New York.

Herkovits, Jean (1977-1978), "Dateline Nigeria: A Black Power", *Foreign Policy* (Washington, DC), no. 29 (Winter), pp. 167-188.

Houser, George M. (1979), *Ending Bank Loans to South Africa*, United Nations Centre Against Apartheid, New York.

— (1982), *The International Impact of the South African Struggle for Liberation*, United Nations Centre Against Apartheid, New York.

Huntington, Samuel P. (1982), "American Ideals and American Institutions", *Political Science Quarterly* (New York), vol.97(1), pp.1-37.

Jackson, Henry F. (1982), *From Congo to Soweto: US Foreign Policy Toward Africa Since 1960*, William Morrow, New York.

Jenkins, Simon (1980), "The Great Evasion, South Africa: A Survey", *The Economist* (London), (June 21), pp.1-30.

Johnson, David (1975), "Troubled Waters for the US Navy", *Africa Report* (New York), vol.20(1), pp.8-10.

Johnson, Willard R. (1973), "United States Foreign Policy Towards Africa", *Africa Today* (Denver), vol.20(1), pp.15-44.

Jones, Alan M. (ed) (1973), *US Foreign Policy in a Changing World: The Nixon Administration, 1969-1973*, David McKay, New York.

Kagan, Donald (1983), "Human Rights, Moralism and Foreign Policy", *The Washington Quarterly* (Cambridge, MA.), vol.12(1), pp.86-95.

Kapur, Ashok (1983), "Carter's Diplomacy and the Indian Ocean Region" in Larry W. Bowman and Ian Clark (eds), *The Indian Ocean in Global Politics*, Young India, New Delhi.

Kennedy, Edward M. (1969), *Congressional Record*, June 9.

Kissinger, Henry (1974), *American Foreign Policy*, W.W. Norton, New York.

--- (1976a), "Secretary Kissinger's News Conference", *Department of State Bulletin*, vol.74 (1925).

--- (1976b), "United States Policy in Southern Africa", *Department of State Bulletin*, vol.74 (1927).

--- (1976c), "United States and Africa", *Department of State Bulletin*, vol.74 (1928).

--- (1976d), "Secretary Kissinger Reports to Congress on his Visit to Latin America, West Europe and Africa", *Department of State Bulletin*, vol.75 (1933).

--- (1976e), "The United States and Africa: Strengthened Ties for an Era of Challenge", *Department of State Bulletin*, vol.75 (1939).

--- (1976f), "Secretary Kissinger's News Conference", *Department of State Bulletin*, vol.75 (1944).

--- (1976g), "The Challenges of Africa", *Department of State Bulletin*, vol.75 (1943).

--- (1976h), "Secretary Kissinger's News Conference", *Department of State Bulletin*, vol.75 (1952).

--- (1981a), *Years of Upheaval*, Vikas, New Delhi.

--- (1981b), *For the Record: Selected Statements 1977-1980*, Weidenfeld and Nicholson, London.

Kucharsky, David (1976), *The Man From Plains: The Mind and Spirit of Jimmy Carter*, Harper and Row, New York.

Lake, Anthony (1979), "Address to the Conference on United States Foreign Policy in Africa", *Department of State Bulletin*, vol.79 (2022).

Leacacos, John P. (1971-1972), "Kissinger's Apparat", *Foreign Policy* (Washington, DC), no.5, pp.3-27.

Leach, Graham (1987), *South Africa: No Easy Path to Peace*, Methuen, London.

Legum, Colin (1976), "The Soviet Union, China and the West in Southern Africa", *Foreign Affairs* (New York), vol.54(4), pp.745-762.

--- (1978), "The USSR and Africa: The African Environment", *Problems of Communism* (Washington, DC), vol.27(1), pp.1-19.

Leighton, Neil O. (1976), "A Perspective on Fundamental Change in Southern Africa: Lusaka–Before and Beyond", *Africa Today* (Denver), vol.2(3), pp.17-24.

LeMelle, Tilden J. (1972), "Race, International Relations, US Foreign Policy and the African Liberation Struggle", *Journal of Black Studies* (Newbury Park), vol.3(1), pp.95-109.

Lipson, Leslie (1964), *The Democratic Civilisation*, Oxford University Press, London.

Lockwood, Edgar (1974), "National Security Study Memorandum 39 and the Future of United States Policy Toward Southern Africa", *Issue* (Waltham), vol.4(3), pp.63-72.

--- (1977), "The Future of the Carter Policy Toward Southern Africa", *Issue* (Waltham), vol.7(4), pp.11-15.

Lukacs, John (1984), *Outgrowing Democracy: A History of the United States in the Twentieth Century*, Wiley Eastern, New Delhi.

Magubane, Bernard M. (1979), *The Political Economy of Race and Class in South Africa*, Monthly Review Press, New York.

Mandela, Nelson (1994), *Long Walk to Freedom*, Little, Brown and Co., London.

Marable, Manning (1985), *Black American Politics: From the Washington Marches to Jesse Jackson*, Verso, London.

Marcum, John (1976), "Lessons of Angola", *Foreign Affairs* (New York), vol.54(3), pp.407-425.

Martin, David and Johnson, Phyllis (1981), *The Struggle for Zimbabwe: The Chimurenga War*, Faber and Faber, London.

McHenry, Donald F. (1978), "Policy Alternatives in Southern Africa", *Worldview* (New York), vol.21(6), pp.34-36.

Mitchell, Clarence, M. (1975), "United States Discusses Human Rights in South Africa", *Department of State Bulletin*, vol.73 (1905).

Mondale, Walter (1977), "Vice President Mondale's News Conference", *Department of State Bulletin*, vol.76 (1982).

Moore, J.D.L. (1987), *South Africa and Nuclear Proliferation: South Africa's Nuclear Capabilities and Intentions in the Context of International Non-Proliferation Policies*, Macmillan, London.

Moose, Richard (1980), "United States Policy Toward South Africa", *Department of State Bulletin*, vol.80 (2040).

Morris, Roger (1977), *Uncertain Greatness: Henry Kissinger and American Foreign Policy*, Quartet Books, London.

Moynihan, Daniel Patrick (1979), *A Dangerous Place*, Allied, Bombay.

Myers III, Desaix and Liff, David M. (1980), "The Press of Business", *Foreign Policy* (Washington, DC), no.38, pp.143-163.

Myrdal, Gunnar (1962), *An American Dilemma: The Negro Problem and American Democracy*, Harper and Row, New York.

Nagorski, Andrew (1978), "United States Options vis à vis South Africa" in Jennifer Seymour Whitaker (ed), *Africa and the United States: Vital Interests*, New York University Press, New York.

Newsom, David (1970), "The United Nations, the United States and Africa", Department of State Bulletin, vol.63 (1633).

--- (1972), "United States Government and Business Partners in African Development", *Department of State Bulletin*, vol.66 (1708).

Newsum, H.E. and Abengunrin, Olayiwola (1987), *United States Foreign Policy Towards Southern Africa: Andrew Young and Beyond*, Macmillan, London.

Nielsen, Waldemar A. (1969), *The Great Powers and Africa*, Pall Mall Press, London.

Nixon, Richard (1970), "United States Foreign Policy for the 1970s: A New Strategy for Peace, A Report to Congress", *Department of State Bulletin*, vol.62, 1602.

--- (1971), "United States Foreign Policy for the 1970s: Building for Peace, A Report to Congress", *Department of State Bulletin*, vol.64 (1656).

Noer, Thomas J. (1978), *Briton, Boer and Yankee: The United States and Africa, 1870-1914*, Kent State University Press, Kent, Ohio.

--- (1981), " 'Non-Benign Neglect': The United States and Black Africa in the Twentieth Century" in Gerald K. Haines and J. Samuel Walker (eds), *American Foreign Relations: A Historiographical Review*, Frances Pinter, London.

Nolutshungu, Sam C. (1985), "South African Policy and United States Options in Southern Africa" in Gerald J. Bender, James S. Coleman and Richard L. Sklar (eds), *African Crisis Areas and US Foreign Policy*, University of California Press, Berkeley and Los Angeles.

Nyerere, Julius (1977a), "America and Southern Africa", *Foreign Affairs* (New York), vol.55(4), pp.671-684.

--- (1977b), "The Role and Responsibility of the United States in South Africa and Rhodesia", *The Black Scholar* (Oakland), vol.9(2), pp.40-46.

Osgood, Robert E. (1953), *Ideals and Self-Interest in America's Foreign Relations: The Great Transformation of the Twentieth Century*, The University of Chicago Press, Chicago.

Ottaway, David (1979), "Africa: US Policy Eclipse", *Foreign Affairs* (New York), vol.58(3), pp.637-658.

Oudes, Bruce (1973), "Observations on America's Policy Problems in Southern Africa", *Issue* (Waltham), vol.3(4), pp.26-42.

--- (1975), "The Sacking of the Secretary", *Africa Report* (New York), vol.20(1), pp.17-19.

Patterson, Walter C. (1984), *The Plutonium Business and the Spread of the Bomb*, Wildwood House, London.

Plimpton, Francis T.P. (1961), "Statement to the United Nations General Assembly", *Department of State Bulletin*, vol.44 (1139).

--- (1962), "Statement to the United Nations on the Problem of Apartheid", *Department of State Bulletin*, vol.47 (1221).

Pogrund, Benjamin (1977), "The Anatomy of White Power", *The Atlantic Monthly* (Boston), (October), pp.51-58.

Radu, Michael (1987), "The African National Congress: Cadres and Credo", *Problems of Communism* (Washington, DC), vol.36(4), pp.58-75.

Ramazani, Rouhollah K. (1983), "The Strait of Hormuz: A Global Checkpoint" in Larry W. Bowman and Ian Clark (eds), *The Indian Ocean in Global Politics*, Young India, New Delhi.

Rees, Judith (1985), *Natural Resources: Allocation, Economics and Policy*, Methuen, New York.

Report of Special Study Mission to Southern Africa (1969), House Committee on Foreign Affairs, 91st Congress, First session, Government Printing Office, Washington, DC.

Richelson, Jeffry T. and Ball, Desmond (1985), *The Ties that Bind*, Allen and Unwin, Boston.

Rogers, William D. (1976), "The Search for Peace in Southern Africa", *Department of State Bulletin*, vol.75 (1948).

Rogers, William P. (1969), "United States Foreign Policy: Some Major Issues", *Department of State Bulletin*, vol.60 (1555).

--- (1970a), "Secretary Rogers Visits Africa", *Department of State Bulletin*, vol.62 (1604).

--- (1970b), "The United States and Africa in the Seventies", *Department of State Bulletin*, vol.62 (1608).

Roherty, James M. (1985), "Beyond Limpopo and Zambesi: South Africa's Strategic Horizons" in William L. Dowdy and Russell B. Trood (eds), *The Indian Ocean: Perspectives on a Strategic Arena*, Duke University Press, Durham.

Rothchild, Donald (1973), "Engagement Versus Disengagement in Africa: The Choices for America" in Alan M. Jones (ed), *US Foreign Policy in a Changing World: The Nixon Administration, 1969-1973*, David Mckay, New York.

Scali, John (1974), "United States Votes Against Expulsion of South Africa from the United Nations", *Department of State Bulletin*, vol.71 (1849).

Schlesinger, Jr., Arthur M. (1965), *A Thousand Days: John F. Kennedy in the White House*, Fawcett Crest, New York.

--- (1986), *The Cycles of American History*, Houghton Mifflin, Boston.

Seidman, Ann (1977), "Problems of Industrialization in Africa", Testimony before Subcommittee on Africa, US House of Representatives, *Issue* (Waltham), vol.7(4), pp.23-25.

Shepherd, George W. (1983), "Demilitarization Proposals for the Indian Ocean" in Larry W. Bowman and Ian Clark (eds), *The Indian Ocean in Global Politics*, Young India, New Delhi.

Skinner, Elliot P. (ed) (1986), *Beyond Constructive Engagement: United States Policy Toward Africa*, Paragon House, New York.

Smith, David M. (ed) (1982), *Living Under Apartheid*, George Allen and Unwin, London.

Smith, Robert S. (1971), "The Dilemma of Foreign Investment", *Department of State Bulletin*, vol.64 (1670).

Smith, Timothy H. (1977), "Bank Loans to South Africa: The Case Against 'Business as Usual' ", *Issue* (Waltham), vol.7(1), pp.12-14.

South Africa and United States Foreign Policy (1969), House Committee on Foreign Affairs, 91st Congress, First Session, Government Printing Office, Washington, DC.

South Africa: Time Running Out (1981), University of California Press, Berkeley.

Southern Africa: Proposals for Americans, A Report of a National Policy Panel established by the United Nations Association of the United States of America (1971), New York.

Southern Africa: The Escalation of Conflict (1976), Stockholm International Peace Research Institute, Stockholm.

Spence, J. E. (1983), "South Africa: The World Powers and Southern Africa" in Thomas M. Callaghy (ed), *South Africa in Southern Africa: The Intensifying Vortex of Violence*, Praeger, New York.

Stadler, Alf (1987), *The Political Economy of Modern South Africa*, Croom Helm, London.

Stevenson, Adlai (1963), "The United States Ban on Sale of Arms to South Africa", *Department of State Bulletin*, vol.49 (1261).

Stookey, Robert W. (1975), *America and the Arab States: An Uneasy Encounter*, John Wiley, New York.

Stupak, Ronald J. (1976), *American Foreign Policy: Assumptions, Processes and Projections*, Harper and Row, New York.

Talbot, Stephen (1977), "United States Intervention in Southern Africa: The New Era", *Socialist Revolution* (San Francisco), vol.34, pp.7-28.

The Activities of Transnational Corporations in the Industrial, Mining and Military Sectors of Southern Africa (1980), United Nations Centre on Transnational Corporations, New York.

The Dynamics of World Power: A Documentary History of United States Foreign Policy, 1945-1973, vol. 5 (1973), Chelsea House Publishers, New York.

The Faces of Africa: Diversity and Progress; Represssion and Struggle, Report of Special Study Missions to Africa (1972), House Committee on Foreign Affairs, 92nd Congress, Second Session, Government Printing Office, Washington, DC.

The United States in the United Nations, 1960: A Turning Point (1961), Senate Committee on Foreign Relations, 87th Congress, First Session, Government Printing Office, Washington, DC.

The White House and the Black Continent (1984), Progress Publishers, Moscow.

Tinker, Hugh (1977), *Race, Conflict and International Order: From Empire to United Nations*, Macmillan, London.

Tocqueville, Alexis de (1966), *Democracy in America*, J. P. Mayer and Max Lerner (eds), Harper and Row, New York.

Todd, Daniel (1988), *Defence Industries: A Global Perspective*, Routledge, London.

Transnational Corporations, Activities of Transnational Corporations in Southern Africa: Impact on Financial and Social Structure (1978), United Nations, New York.

Troup, Freda (1972), *South Africa: A Historical Introduction*, Eyre Methuen, London.

Uhling, Mark A. (ed) (1986), *Apartheid in Crisis*, Penguin, Harmondsworth.

Ungar, Sanford J. and Vale, Peter (1986), "Why Constructive Engagement Failed" in Mark A. Unlig (ed), *Apartheid in Crisis*, Penguin, Harmondsworth.

United States Policy Toward South Africa (1980), Hearings Before the Subcommittee on International Economic Policy and Trade, Subcommittee on Africa, and Subcommittee on International Organization, House Committee on Foreign Affairs, 96th Congress, Second Session, Government Printing Office, Washington, DC.

US Business Involvement in Southern Africa (1972), Hearings before the Subcommittee on Africa, House Committee on Foreign Affairs, 92nd Congress, First Session, Part II, Government Printing Office, Washington, DC.

US Economic Expansion: Asia and Africa (1986), USSR Academy of Sciences, Moscow.

Uttley, Garrick (1979-1980), "Globalism or Regionalism: United States Policy Towards Southern Africa", *Adelphi Paper*, no.154, International Institute for Strategic Studies (London), pp.1-36.

Vance, Cyrus (1977a), "The United States and Africa: Building Positive Relations" in Elaine P. Adam (ed), *American Foreign Relations 1977: A Documentary Record*, New York University Press, New York.

--- (1977b), "Sanctions Against South Africa", *Department of State Bulletin*, vol.77 (2004).

--- (1979a), "An Affirmative Approach" in Elaine P. Adam (ed), *American Foreign Relations, 1978: A Documentary Record*, New York University Press, New York.

--- (1979b), "Change in Southern Africa", *Department of State Bulletin*, vol.79 (2024).

Vandenbosch, Amry (1970), *South Africa and the World: The Foreign Policy of Apartheid*, University Press of Kentucky, Lexington.

Venn, Fiona (1986), *Oil Diplomacy in the Twentieth Century*, Macmillan, Basingstoke.

Walters, Ronald E. (1976), "Apartheid and the Atom: The United States and South Africa's Military Potential", *Africa Today* (Denver), vol.23(3), pp.25-35.

Whitaker, Jennifer Seymour (ed) (1978), *Africa and United States: Vital Interests*, New York University Press, New York.

Wilson, Andrew (1975), "Why the United States Titled Towards Vorster", *The Observer* (London), (January 5).

Winchester, Simon (1974), "Dr. Kissinger Slated for African Policy", *Manchester Guardian Weekly* (October 19).

Yost, Charles W. (1963), "The United States Ban on the Sale of Arms to South Africa", *Department of State Bulletin*, vol.49 (1261).

--- (1969), "Statement Before the Security Council", *Department of State Bulletin*, vol.61 (1569).

Young, Andrew (1977), "United States Reiterates Support for Independence of Namibia and Zimbabwe", *Department of State Bulletin*, vol.77 (1985).

--- (1980), "The United States and Africa: Victory for Diplomacy", *Foreign Affairs* (New York), vol.59(3), pp. 648-666.

Index